The Promoter

My sheep hear my voice, and I know them, and they follow me.
—John 10:27 (NKJV)

Ron Meyers

ISBN 978-1-0980-5009-2 (paperback)
ISBN 978-1-0980-5711-4 (hardcover)
ISBN 978-1-0980-5010-8 (digital)

Copyright © 2020 by Ron Meyers

All rights reserved. No part of this publication may be reproduced, distributed, or transmitted in any form or by any means, including photocopying, recording, or other electronic or mechanical methods without the prior written permission of the publisher. For permission requests, solicit the publisher via the address below.

Christian Faith Publishing, Inc.
832 Park Avenue
Meadville, PA 16335
www.christianfaithpublishing.com

Scripture taken from the New King James Version. Copyright © 1982 by Thomas Nelson, Inc. Used by permission. All rights reserved.

Scripture quotations are from The ESV® Bible (The Holy Bible, English Standard Version®), copyright © 2001 by Crossway, a publishing ministry of Good News Publishers. Used by permission. All rights reserved.

Scriptures marked KJV are taken from the KING JAMES VERSION (KJV): KING JAMES VERSION, public domain.

Printed in the United States of America

Dedication

This book is dedicated to my awesome family: Karen, my wife of over 33 years, and my four children, Dawn, Ron II, Ryan, and Jacob, the lights of my life. This book is for the lonely, the broken-hearted, the hopeless, the unloved, and every other person who is searching for purpose, meaning, and peace. Also, it is for my grandchildren who I would like them to know who grandfather was and speak destiny into their life. I am so grateful that God would take me, a chief misfit, and turn my life into a testimony of his goodness, mercy, love, and grace. I hope that the person reading this book will experience restoration, spiritual renewal, and a clear understanding of God's intention for their life.

Acknowledgment

I want to thank Bobbie Sue Fenton for editing this book as well as taking my story and turning it into an enjoyable read.

Foreword

This story was written based on actual situations that did occur. The first half of the book is my life as a promoter of sex, drugs, greed, and anything I could make a buck at. The second half of the book is about my life after I had a supernatural encounter with Jesus. Today I am a promoter of love, peace, purpose, passion, and destiny. I gave God the glory for my success in going down both roads in my life. Both the one it took me time to realize I shouldn't be going down, as well as the one I should, for without the first road, I never would have appreciated the second. Some of my stories may surprise you. But some of you may find they are not so different from your own. For those of you who found God and turned quickly to Him, you'll probably find a few moments where you will gasp and turn white, as it took me a while to "get it." God had to pursue me, and it took 40 years before I surrendered.

For those of you who are looking for a book about a "real Christian" (the term used on a website I stumbled upon one day to describe one such as I who struggled with the World), it doesn't get any more real than this. For those who weren't so hard-headed, please don't misunderstand, or take offense—I know you are just as "real" a Christian as I. For no one is truly a Christian until they surrender, and entirely turn to God whether it takes them 4 seconds or 40 years. Not understanding just what God was all about or how He does things, I had an awful lot to learn, and I thank God He was patient enough to wait for the lightbulb to come on. I was probably much worse than I appeared in this book.

The greatest lesson I believe that you will take away is that no matter what you have done or haven't done or how messed up you might think you are, you can't be too broken for God. If He can forgive a sinner like me, He most certainly can forgive you. We don't find God, He finds us. And once He decides you belong to Him; He will never give you up—no matter who you are or what you've done.

As you are about to discover, brought up in a home without God forced me to fend for myself from a young age. I made some bad choices, running with the devil well into adulthood. Greed, drugs, doubt, fear, financial ruin, and so much loss—you name it—I dealt with the hell in my life in the craziest ways. I searched for peace and purpose each day and usually only found more hell. I was in a constant wrestling match with God from the first time I heard His voice until I finally surrendered.

It all changed in a plea of desperation one morning when I called out to God for help from the floor of my closet after a failed attempt to end my life as a mere boy. It was that day that God introduced Himself to me. Little did I know, it would be the beginning of a life-long relationship. Even when I didn't know Him when I gave my life to Him in 6th grade, He began working in my life, drawing me toward Him until that day, I finally surrendered. As I mentioned, I still had a lot of kinks to work out before I really "got it." But even through my worst, He never left me or gave up on me. God guided me through my moments of stubborn pride, frustration, and foolishness until I finally understood, and had the hell blown out of my life. Are things perfect in my life today? Of course not! But I don't have the wrestling matches I had with God in my early days nor rely on my wisdom anymore, but instead, I follow Him, relying on Him to guide me, and strive every day knowing that He is always with me, even when I fall.

It is my prayer that my real-life experiences and hard-earned wisdom, as portrayed in this book through my inner struggles as I learned to trust and rely on God, will be able to help you learn to trust his guidance in your own life. I prayed feverishly before and during the writing of this book. I hope that this book releases a fresh anointing of God's love, mercy, and grace into your life. As God did in my life, I pray He will meet you where you are and lead you into the place where He begins shaping you into the person you initially were created become. Then, you will start to hear His still quiet voice, His voice of truth, love, empowerment, encouragement, and direction, and I promise you, it will change your life.

Table of Contents

Part 1:   I'll Show Them
- Chapter 1:   The Voice..15
  - It's Not Always What It Seems..............17
  - The Meeting 21
  - The Hoods 23
  - Caught 26
- Chapter 2:   Mind Over Money..................................29
  - Dodgeball..31
  - The Chosen 32
  - Henry's Hamburgers 34
- Chapter 3:   Love Held Me Together..........................40
  - Gas and a Girl..41
  - The Date...42
  - Meet the Parents....................................45
  - The Kozy Inn..47
  - Welcome to Adulthood 48
  - So Long Iowa 49
  - You're in the Air Force Now!..................52
  - Tattoos Tell No Tales 54
  - Love Me Say Good-bye 56
  - Biloxi, Mississippi...................................57
- Chapter 4:   Meet Mr. Mom 58
  - The Storms Come 60
  - And the Beat Goes On 63

	Still Waters 66
	WWW Brenda 68
Chapter 5:	It's Showtime! 69
	Showtime! 71
Chapter 6:	The Chicago Knockers 75
	The Dedeaux Delusion 76
	Mud On My Face 79
	Gone 82
Chapter 7:	I Need a Miracle 85
	Put Up Your Dukes 88
	A Way Out 90
	Attitude Adjustment 91
	The Crawfish Festival 93
Chapter 8:	Out of the Frying Pan and Into the Fire 96
	My Day in Court 98
Chapter 9:	My Step of Faith 100
Chapter 10:	The Power of an Idea 104
Chapter 11:	And the Devil Had Dimples 108
	The Invisible Fish 114
Chapter 12:	The Monster Arm Wrestling Machine 115
Chapter 13:	The Death of My Lawyer 117
Chapter 14:	Music and Merry Christmas 120
	Christmas Fair and Craft Sale Comes to Biloxi Coliseum 121
Chapter 15:	Protests and A Hurricane 124
	The Beer Was Flowing, and So Was the Money ... 124
	Here Come the Pesky Christians! 125
Chapter 16:	I Showed Them! 127
	October 6, 1984, Marquee Cover Story 127
	The Wall Cracked 129
Chapter 17:	Facing fear in the Face 130
	Hurricane Elena 132

Chapter 18: I Get Married Again...134
    Dancing Déjà vu...135
Chapter 19: The Swimsuit Calendar and More Protests..........137
    The Girls of the Gulf Coast Calendar is
    Finished, and It is a Beauty!.................................139
Chapter 20: Here They Come, After the Christmas Show!......141
    Christmas City USA Debuts on
    November 11–12, 1988 143
    Christmas City Hits the Road! 144
Chapter 21: Lord, My Son Needs a Miracle............................146
Chapter 22: My Conscience Was Pricked................................149
    The Warning..151
Chapter 23: My Mom Died...154
Chapter 24: My Party's Over!..156
Chapter 25: The Day I Surrendered..160
    A New Person..163

Part 2:   From Beer to Bibles
Chapter 26: The Birth of Cross 2 Success & My Son..............167
    Cross 2 Success..169
    Emmitt & Wanda Pillault 170
Chapter 27: Testimony of a Columbine Dad 174
Chapter 28: The Warehouse Church..177
    The Least of Them..178
    My Favorite Night...180
    A Change Is Coming...181
Chapter 29: The Brownsville Revival 183
    September 29, 2000 185
Chapter 30: Time to Open the Tackle Box with My
    Brand-New Lures...188
    Outreaches and the Angel....................................190
    Blood on the Tracks
    March 25, 2001 191

  Spirit Fest
  April 1, 2001–2004 192
  God and Country
  July 4, 2001 194
  There Were Skeptics! 195
  I Closed the Church Services 196
Chapter 31: The Announcement that Shocked the Coast 198
Chapter 32: Some of My Favorite Stories from the
  Radio Days 203
  Ashley Smith 203
  Eutychus—The Band Perry 204
  Brittany Waddell—Britt Nicole 205
  Mercy Me 205
  Local Artists of the Week 206
  The Ten-Thousand-Foot Jump 207
  The Calendar Controversy 207
Chapter 33: I Become General Manager of the Station 210
Chapter 34: A Storm Is Coming
  KATRINA! 212
  The Equalizer 217
  Here Come the Campers 218
  My Contractor 220
  The Rest of the Story 221
Chapter 35: Terminated! 223
  The Loss Was Worse than Death 224
  Perfect Timing 225
Chapter 36: God Sent My Dad to Me 227
  The Power of Love 229
  For We Know Not What Day 230
  Dad's Last Wishes 231
  The Election 232
  The Last Good-bye 233

Part 1

I'll Show Them

Chapter 1

The Voice

> Pain insists upon being attended to. God
> whispers to us in our pleasures, speaks in
> our consciences, but shouts in our pains. It is
> his megaphone to rouse a deaf world.
> —C.S. Lewis

Growing up, I was one of those people who was just always in trouble. I didn't have to look for it, though I admit, I often did; it just seemed to follow me. I seemed to have just come into the world that way.

"Alright, guys! Get to your bases and let's PLAY BALL!" shouted the coach as he straightened his ball cap to keep out the blinding sun.

A herd of small, mostly 10-year-old boys raced onto the field, leaving a cloud of dust in their wake. A handsome statue of a man standing 6'6" and 230 pounds with piercing green eyes and a strong square chin, Ron Meyers Sr. presented a formidable appearance to those who met him, to say the least; especially when you didn't come up much past his belt loops. "Whoa there, Slugger, where do you think you're going? Hit the bench! You can play in a little bit." I heard him say as I found his hand suddenly on my chest. Immediately, as always, my shoulders drooped, my head dropped, and I trudged my way to the bench. The coaches never let me play. None of them did, not even my own Dad.

To be fair, I kind of understood it. I was awful; I mean, REALLY bad. The ball just seemed to magically go around me, through my legs, over my head, everywhere but in my glove. However, there was this one time I did get to play the entire game.

"Ben! Ben! Get the phone! I can't get my gloves off!" Ms. White said as the petite redhead fumbled with her dripping wet yellow rubber gloves anxiously over a sink full of dishes.

A prematurely balding man with a bit of a belly mumbled as he set his cigar into the ashtray on the top shelf of the end table next to him while simultaneously slamming his newspaper into his lap impatiently.

"Ben!" Ms. White exclaimed again from the kitchen.

"Hold your horses! I'm moving as fast as I can!" he growled, mumbled again, then reached over the arm of his well-worn dark mustard colored tweed recliner to the lower shelf of the end table and picked up the receiver of the black rotary dialed telephone. "Hello? White's residence, who's speaking?" He looked up impatiently as Helen White came into the room. Her gaze met his, her eyebrows raised with inquisitiveness as she dried her hands off with the red and white checkered dish towel she'd gotten as a bonus out of the last box of detergent she'd bought. He centered his attention back to the phone call.

"Uh-huh, uh-huh, okay. Thank you for calling, good-bye," Mr. White set the receiver back onto the hook clumsily as he raised his paper once again.

Ms. White knew he had picked up his cigar because a giant mushroom-shaped cloud of smoke hovered above the newspaper. She waved the air with her dishrag in feigned disdain. "Well?" she inquired.

At that moment, a young boy dressed in a baseball uniform walked up and stood beside her while ruffling the ears of a small wiggly beagle puppy clutched in his arms. What his dad would say next would have him looking up at his mom with grave disappointment.

"No ball game tonight."

THE PROMOTER

It's Not Always What It Seems

Meanwhile, back at the Meyers household, Ron gently placed the heavy receiver down on the hook of the telephone, careful not to make a sound. He looked around one last time to make sure no one saw him using the phone, picked up his bat from the corner of the hallway where he'd leaned it before calling the Whites and walked casually into the living room just in time to see his Dad stepping in through the back door. "Okay! If you're coming with me, get in the car! We're going to be late!" Ron smiled as he ran for the car.

On the outside, things couldn't have appeared any more perfect. My life looked like it had fallen right out of a Norman Rockwell painting. I grew up in the heart of middle America suburbia in a beautiful city called Cedar Rapids, Iowa, which is rich in history. The Cedar River flowed right through the center of this multicultural city with its cutting-edge schools, blocks upon blocks of beautiful multi-story buildings, and sidewalks lined with storefronts. Surrounded by several perfectly manicured parks, the city also had an abundance of recreational lakes located nearby. At night it was full of lights and sound, with plenty to do and see. It was an exciting time and place to live!

Nine of us lived in the Northwest side of town, where most of the middle-class lived, in a cookie-cutter, 1200 square foot, one bath, three-bedroom row house built sometime after World War II. Each one had a little yard and a patio. My three brothers and I did everything together, and my three sisters—they did their own thing. In the evenings, most folks would sit in the yard and greet one another as many took their evening strolls. In fall, we would rake up piles of leaves and have bonfires in the street, and everyone would gather around to enjoy the warmth and each other's company. Weather permitting, we kids filled the roads on bicycles with playing cards clipped to our spokes with clothespins so that they made a loud clacking sound when the wheels turned. If we weren't in school, most parents had no idea where their children were until the streetlights came on at dusk. It never crossed anyone's mind to worry because there was no need. Everyone knew everybody.

On Sundays, we'd go to my maternal Grandmother's house for Sunday dinner in Fairfax, a small farm town nearby. Together with all my cousins, there were at least 25 of us kids! My mother came from an extensive family of nine children, so the family grouped in one place was massive, loud, and boisterous. Grandpa would have us kids stand in the middle of the yard, and laughing, he would throw handfuls of change up into the air. I remember how it glittered in the sun as it showered down onto the ground. I can still almost hear the peals of laughter among us as we'd dive into the grass and scramble for the money. Then, like a wild pack of young wolves, we'd run to the store for penny candy or to the Dairy Queen for ice cream and then run all over town playing hide-and-go-seek! We thought it tremendously exciting to lay coins on the tracks then lie in wait for the train to come and flatten them. And on Easter, we'd all load up to go to a nearby German town—Amana, Iowa. Why yes, it is where Amana appliances got their name! We would eat at one of the many excellent German restaurants there. It seemed like an ideal way to grow up, and this part of it was. It truly was.

As for my parents—my Dad was the outgoing type, one of those charismatic people to whom people just seemed drawn. With his good looks and magnetic personality, he probably should have been in sales. He worked as a custodian in the schools by day, and usually in Doctor's offices doing the same job at night. He wasn't particularly demonstrative and could be stern, but I think it was because of the significant burden he had on his shoulders, raising such a large family. I believe that burden weighed on him so, that often that's all he had on his mind. The typical workaholic, it wasn't unusual for Dad to hold three jobs just to make sure he could adequately provide for his family. Needless-to-say, we didn't see him much. Occasionally, he'd bring us to work with him when he had to clean the school in summer or on weekends. He would have us, boys, scrubbing floors, and cleaning desks while he leaned back in the teacher's lounge listening to Paul Harvey on the radio. He would reward us each with a bottle of Mountain Dew and a bag of Fritos, a price which we thought in those days had been certainly worth the effort.

THE PROMOTER

My Mom was a pretty and petite woman, always prim and proper. In her world, everything had its place, and it, and you, best, be in it. She kept Dad's little army going with strict discipline and made sure that we knew how to keep things ship-shape. We weren't allowed to linger in the kitchen, and we best not touch the refrigerator. If we wanted a drink of water, we boys knew that's what the hose outside was for. If the weather was sunny and chores completed, it was expected of us to be out in the sunshine. Whether boy or girl, we each knew how to clean, take care of our clothes, and our appearance. She made sure that we had manners and were always polite in public, respecting our elders and saying, "yes, Mam," and "no Mam," or "Sir," as the situation required and to always say "please" and "thank you." She made sure it was drilled into our heads, "Appearance is everything!" She had high expectations for all of us and had her cap set that we were going to follow along her path, which she had all planned out for us. Thus, her training was so complete that to the outsider, we seemed like the picture-perfect family.

Yet, as perfect as this little picture appeared, as is often the case behind closed doors with the shades drawn, it couldn't have been further from the truth. I got in trouble—a LOT. I was hyper, curious, and into everything, and no one had any time or patience for my antics. It was expected of me to sit still, speak when spoken to, and to be seen, not heard. Because of the sheer flood of criticism, which seemed to pour down on my person most of the time, often, I didn't feel like I even 'fit' in my own family. I was the proverbial black sheep, the oddball, unwanted, and unloved. Sometimes, I was sure I brought a lot of it on myself. But quite often, I thought if they were just a little more patient with me, they'd see I wasn't as awful as they accused me of being. I was whipped with a belt by my Dad, sometimes within an inch of my life, when I'd get into trouble. In my mom's case—I got the shoe. Not a regular flat-heeled shoe, mind you, but the high heel shoe right on the top of my noggin. Sass my mom? Whack! I'd see stars for two days!

As you might imagine, my self-worth was virtually non-existent most of the time, and the only way I could escape my mother's disapproval and the terror that loomed inside my mind was to daydream.

So, I became a dreamer. I considered how my life might have gone had things been different, most of all, of what I was going to do in the future. I wasn't sure what I was going to be, as my thoughts on the matter changed daily depending on what influenced me at the time. But whatever I became, a tiny part of me believed that I was going to be great at it! That small flame even I didn't understand, but jealously guarded, told me that I knew I was meant for something different, something that would make me stand out from the crowd and make a difference. I felt that if I could live through this, that no matter what anyone said: parents, teachers, enemies, whatever; someday I WOULD amount to something! Instead of cowering and backing down, my defense mechanism became to look at the offending party straight in the eye (even though most of the time, I admit, they were stinging with angry tears I refused to shed) and yell at the top of my voice, "You just wait and see! I am going to be famous one day!" They would just laugh and call me crazy with their eyes still deadlocked with mine so that I knew I was looking right into their soul. I was sure that they positively believed I was utterly, totally, and completely worthless.

Even though I did my best to hide it, I was a sensitive soul, easily offended, so a part of me believed what they said about me as I never felt like I quite measured up anyway. When I was angry, often, the "flame" I spoke of seemed far away. Sometimes, so far away, that my "defense mechanism" came out sounding hollow even to my ears. Thus, the disapproval of others for any infraction, no matter how minor, I still took incredibly personally. Often, I wondered if there wasn't a big red target painted on my back. It seemed to me that in the eyes of those around me, nothing I ever did was ever quite good enough, no matter how I tried. I remember cringing whenever I thought I had done an excellent job, quite often instead of eliciting praise; infallibly, someone would pipe up as to how so-in-so could do it better. Of course, this usually left me feeling devastated. There just wasn't a lot of encouragement, love, or affection in our house. I never remembered getting hugs or kisses growing up. With so many mouths to feed, maybe our parents felt it was enough just putting a roof over our heads, clothes on our backs and food in our bellies. Whatever their reasoning, this deep feeling of worthlessness and hopelessness and the deep unmet need to feel wanted and loved worked together to brew the perfect storm in me. It culminated somewhere in my mind to the conclusion that maybe I just wasn't worthy of love. When one is told they are worthless often and long enough, that person will eventually believe it.

The Meeting

One morning, just before daybreak, I awoke all alone in my room I shared with my three brothers after spending a restless night feeling sorry for myself. As I usually did things, I made up my mind at that moment to do something about it. My brothers had all spent the night with friends, and I just decided I couldn't take it anymore. I was utterly lost. I didn't know who I was and no longer cared anymore, convinced that no one else did, so why should I? The darkness inside of me had finally taken over the last bit of what hope I had clung to that things might change, and I had just decided that the world would be better off without me. Maybe they would all be sorry when I was gone; perhaps they wouldn't. But either way, the pain would finally end.

It's amazing how time seems to slow down when you decide to do something stupid. You become acutely aware of everything, every sound, or the lack of them. Everyone in the house was still asleep. Though it was still dark, the streetlight gave just enough light through my window that I could see, causing long, creepy shadows to stretch across the walls. I could hear the pops and snaps of the house as the coming morning warmed it. The faucet that my youngest sister was ever leaving dripping in the bathroom. After all, she couldn't quite reach the handles seemed incredibly loud. Even the ticking of the clock in the living room seemed to be trying to tell on me. The house still smelled like a mixture of last night's supper, coffee, and the stuff with which mom dusted the furniture.

I got up slowly from my bunk and pulled my belt out of the pants I had worn the day before, which I had slung across the post of the top bunk. Quietly, I walked across the coil rug to the other set of bunk beds and picked up the small footstool. Shaking off my brother's dirty socks he'd left there in a hurry to get to a friend's house, I thought about the trouble he would be in when my mother saw them, so I kicked them under the bed to save him a beating. Ever so quietly, I carried the stool to the closet. I bent down and placed it on the floor of the closet where usually my brother's shoes would be, and gingerly climbed onto the stool. I wrapped the leather belt tightly around my neck and reaching up, attached the other end to the clothing rod.

Just in case, I thought that maybe I should say something to God before I did it. I wasn't particularly religious or anything as growing up, my family never talked about Jesus. Though being Catholic, we did attend church together on Christmas and Easter. Out of seven children, I being the next to the oldest; I was the only one that went to a Catholic school. In second grade, the public-school principal said I was disruptive and a problem student. As I stood there on that stool, I remembered how the old geezer had looked self-righteously over his wire-rimmed glasses. He had told my parents that the only way I could return to school was to go to the University of Iowa and undergo psychiatric exams. I guess he wanted to make sure I had a brain. My parents were told that my IQ was higher than average and that I was bored with school.

My parents' remedy was to pull me out of public school and place me in Saint Jude's Grade School, convinced the nuns and priest could keep me in line. They were wrong. Within the first two weeks of school, I found myself in the principal's office for using profanity on the playground. I can still see the sister unwrapping the bar of soap with the word "Maxine" printed on the wrapper, and even now, I can still taste the bubbles coming out of my mouth. My parents weren't happy with me, especially when they asked me why, I answered them, "I only said the words you say!" I felt the darkness inside of me, weigh a little heavier as I remembered that day. Even as a 2nd grader, I was a screw-up. Even so, I said the Lord's Prayer and a Hail Mary, and then I did it. At eleven years old, I jumped off the footstool.

The belt instantly tightened around my neck as I hung there for a moment, causing me to cough. Then it happened. The entire clothes rod came loose from the wall dumping me in a heap on the floor with the stool, and all my clothes fell on my head. As I sat there at the bottom of my closet with my bellbottom jeans draped over my face, I knew my mom was right; I was a failure. I couldn't even kill myself right. Then it dawned on me that surely my parents must have heard the racket. If I woke my mother up, I knew she'd be in there straight away with her shoe to beat me over the head with it. I may not have killed myself, but I was pretty sure when she came in and saw this mess, she'd complete the job. I strained to listen for any sound that might warn me I'd awakened them. Though I wasn't quite sure how the house was utterly silent, I couldn't even hear the water dripping anymore. Somehow, I hadn't awakened anyone in the house!

Then I heard a voice. It wasn't a person's voice. I'm not sure how to explain it, but it was real and clear and coming from somewhere inside of me. It was just as audible as if someone were in the room speaking to me! It was soft, gentle, loving, and said, "Ronnie, don't hurt yourself. I love you, and I have a plan for you." I looked around just to make sure I was alone. I felt a little scared, confused, and relieved all at the same time. I knew it had to be Jesus talking to me since Sister Mary Katherine had told the class at school that Jesus knew our voice, and we would know His voice. As I sat there in the dark, wondering if that had just happened, I felt something I hadn't felt for a very long time. Hope. I realized that Jesus had saved my life that day. Though I would still have a long row to hoe, that was the last time I ever wanted to hurt myself.

The Hoods

As the seventh grade was approaching, my parents considered moving me to a private school because even the nuns couldn't control me. The last straw came when I stood up in religion class and asked, "Why do we pray to Mary and not Jesus?" That trip to the principal's office earned me detention. Little did I know at the time, that very question was a harbinger of things to come.

That night, I overheard my parents talking. "Dear, I just don't know what I'm going to do with that troublemaker! No matter what I tell him to do, he just seems Hell-bent on doing the exact opposite! I've never seen anything like it! I'm at my wit's end," my mother's stressed voice drifted through the closed bedroom door. Even though I couldn't see her, I could picture her animated face, and I knew that she was chain-smoking. She always did when aggravated with me.

"Now Beverly, I'm sorry, but I've already told you, we just don't have the money to send him to private school. It was all we could do to send him to St. Jude's. He's just going to have to go to a public school," my father replied matter-of-factly. He was probably smoking as well. I seemed to have that effect on both of them. I remember going to bed, crying myself to sleep, just thinking, *Why me?*

After that morning, when I had heard God speak to me, it had become a habit to talk to Jesus. Talking to Jesus gave me peace in a chaotic world, and somehow, it always made me feel like everything would be okay. I spoke to him about everything, even, in my innocent ignorance, when I was hiding behind the bleachers at school smoking cigarettes, I'd snuck from my parents. I also talked to him about the times I snuck out of the house to meet up with my "juvenile delinquent" friends, as my mother called them. I'd met them after moving to public school. Though I still had a lot to learn about God, I never tried to hide anything from Him. After all, I reasoned, the sisters had told us that God could see everything, so it would have been kind of silly of me to try.

I believe I mentioned that I would do just about anything to attract attention. My life of crime started with candy bars that would somehow mysteriously find their way into my pockets on the few occasions my mom took me with her shopping. I'd take them to school, stash them in my locker, and sell them to all the sweets deprived kids for a tidy profit. I was the school hero. This behavior became amplified when I left Catholic school and re-entered the public-school system. It was no surprise that I always seemed to gravitate towards the outcasts and the misfits, feeling that I fit into this category quite perfectly. I felt more comfortable with them than I had with the Catholic religious crowd. I felt the three kids who became my 'partners in crime', were from my side of the tracks: kids of blue-collar workers, not the white bread boys of privilege I was raised to believe I was. They, too, came from troubled pasts of abuse and broken homes. My mother called them 'juvenile delinquents.' However, these weren't just juvenile delinquents; they were the "gold stars of juvenile delinquents." I found the family I didn't have at home in my pals Kenny, Sonny, and Lucas. In them, I found the affection, acceptance, and camaraderie I longed for—my gang, mi amigos! With them, I was somebody!

With public school, I'd started a tradition of three-day suspensions, which would continue from the seventh grade every year until the tenth grade. I was still gravitating toward anything that brought me attention. But by this time, my parents had pretty much given up on me though I was still often the recipient of a healthy 'whipping' or 'shoeing,' depending on how you want to look at it from my mom. At such times, she never failed to remind me of how I was nothing but trouble, just a stupid kid that would never amount to anything and that my bags would be packed and sitting at the front door when I graduated—that is if I graduated which was fine with me. Needless-to-say, I spent as little time at home as possible, which brought a lot more peace to all parties involved.

My gang and I would do the usual stupid things you would expect wayward teenage boys to do, like throwing snowballs at passing cars and counting it lucky if we made someone mad enough actually to chase us. We got a reputation for being tough and cool, smoking cigarettes and became as thick as thieves—mostly petty thieves. We were the bad boys that your mother told you about and to avoid. But boy! How the girls loved to look at us! For the most part, we were harmless enough. The exception to this, borrowing a car one evening without permission from one of the school bus drivers who had left his keys in his car. We took it joyriding several miles from town, but on that day, most of the roads were still mud and gravel, and it had been raining all day. We took turns driving, and after speeding down one slippery way, we succeeded in skidding off to end up hopelessly stuck in a muddy ditch. After several hours of trying to free the car from the mud, we gave up and ended up walking the five miles back to town in the pouring rain. That was the one, and the only time we took anything more substantial than a piggy bank.

We didn't steal as much for the money as for the glory. We'd sneak onto school buses during games and went through the girl's purses, taking any money we found. We broke into houses—okay—not precisely broke in, just entered. One of our gang had a paper route, and in those days, one collected payments in person. If the customer weren't home, we'd try the front doorknob. If it was unlocked, we went into the house. Being teenage boys, we'd always do the most practical thing first—we'd head straight for the refrigerator. Never being allowed to have anything that wasn't put on our plates at home, we were always insatiably hungry. Our hunger satisfied; we'd check the kid's rooms for piggy banks. We didn't take anything else. We wouldn't have known what to do with a tv or a stereo system.

The next morning was our moment of fame. We'd gather around the nearest radio and listen for the local radio station to broadcast the crimes that occurred in our city overnight. When we heard the address of the house we had entered the night before, we'd laugh and cheer with excitement! We had made the news! We were genuinely shocked at the dishonesty of some people. Often, the broadcast stated that the thieves had stolen expensive items, and we'd look at each other dumbfounded, shouting in unison to no one in particular, "Liars!" I guess they'd come up with such accusations for the insurance money. We never thought about getting into any real trouble, as it was just a game to us. Could we break into houses without getting caught? It was fun listening for our escapades on the morning police report. We never had any intentions of hurting anyone, and never looked for anything else in the house other than food and piggy banks. It was all in fun until one night, a family arrived home early.

Caught

Kenny and I, we were helping ourselves to a turkey sandwich, Lucas was in the bathroom, and Sonny was checking the kid's rooms for piggy banks. I was halfway through one of the best turkey sandwiches I'd ever eaten, piled high with everything but the kitchen sink when I stopped in mid-chew as my heart sank into my stomach. "Hey, Kenny, is that car slowing down?" I asked, lowering my sandwich onto the plate as I listened intently.

Kenny poked his head from around the refrigerator door with a pickle in his mouth and listened. His eyes widened as the pickle dropped from his mouth. "Holy Crap! We're busted!" he shouted as we heard the engine of a car pull into the driveway, and the light from the headlights came through the thin white curtains of the living room window, hitting first the ceiling then briefly illuminating our hijinks in the kitchen. "Leave it!" he shouted at me as I had started to put the lid back on the mayonnaise jar half in shock. He shoved me in the direction of the back door as Lucas, a wiry, redheaded kid, came barreling out of the bathroom with his pants half down, trying to pull them up. He halfway stumbled, half hopped to the back door where Sonny was already fumbling with the locks trying to get the back door open.

"Why on earth did they lock the back door when the front door was left wide open?" Sonny cried.

"Just hurry up and get the thing open! We got to get out of here!" Kenny whispered loudly.

The back door finally flew open just as the front door opened, and we practically fell over one another trying to get out of the house as the lights came on and we heard voices in the living room behind us. Lucas shrieked like a little girl not far behind me as we ran through the back yard. I know I set an Olympic record that night! Running like madmen through one back yard to the next, we leaped chain link fences and didn't stop until we were far away. After almost being apprehended, that was the end of our adventurous reign of terror on refrigerators and kid's piggy banks.

In addition to my brief career as milk money, piggy bank, and sandwich burglar, I was also the class clown, doing anything to make my classmates laugh. It didn't take them long to figure out all they had to do was dare me to do something, and I would do it. Some of those things were rather hurtful, like telling our homeroom teacher who was humpbacked that she looked like a turtle. However, it never stopped me. Even though I got sent to the office, it was worth it to me for the laughter and attention. Like any juvenile delinquent worth their salt, during breaks between classes, we went outside on campus and smoked pot. I always made it back in time for class, though a little hungry and confused, but never-the-less, there in body, not sure on the mind part.

Chapter 2
Mind Over Money

> But the Lord said to Samuel, "Do not look at his appearance or at his physical stature, because I have refused him. For the Lord does not see as man sees; for man looks at the outward appearance, but the Lord looks at the heart."
> —1 Samuel 16:7 (NKJV)

Though I still found plenty of ways to get into trouble, after nearly getting caught, I'd pretty much quit most of my five-finger discount ways by now. As I had mentioned before, my ill-gotten gains had never been about the money; it had always just been about glory. I believe I said my father worked three jobs to support the family, so if I wanted money, I had to earn it. I didn't get anything extra from home as with nine mouths to feed, everything that came in the house was to keep a roof over our heads. So, I did the usual things most kids do to try to earn money. I mowed lawns in the summer, shoveled driveways in the winter, sold greeting cards door to door, and I even had a *TV Guide* route. TV Guides were these little books with all the television listings in them which were delivered to your door each week just like a newspaper.

In the summer of '71, I was fourteen years old and had made up my mind I wanted to work as a hawker at the Veterans Memorial Stadium, home of the Cedar Rapids Cardinals, minor league baseball team. I realized that if I wanted things to change, I had to take control of my own life by my willingness to go the extra mile. The extra mile ended up being four miles—round trip, on foot. I had been saving my money to buy a car, so I could finally escape and move out of the house, but as of that day, I hadn't quite had enough saved up just yet.

Twice already, I had walked the two miles through the city to the stadium in the blistering summer heat, soaked to the bone in my sweat, in hopes of being chosen to hawk concessions. And, twice I walked home unchosen, but undefeated. The third time I set out toward the stadium, it began to rain. I welcomed the relief though it didn't last long. As the sun started to set over the river, the comfort quickly turned into a sauna as the hot streets and sidewalks began to send the rain back where it came from in clouds of steam. The seven-year locusts were out that year, and their loud whirring filled the air. I focused on the path in front of me, my determination that this time I would be chosen growing with every step. It was the home game between our team and the Quincy Cubs, the strongest team to beat in the league. I knew the stadium would be packed with hungry and thirsty patrons more than willing to part with some cash for a cold pop on such a steamy day, and I was determined to be one of those in the stands ready and willing to take their money.

Our team had been doing great that year, and though it was a whole hour before the pitch, just as I'd anticipated, the crowd in the stadium was already one of the biggest I think I'd ever seen. The noise of their moving about and talking was deafening. I cut across the small side field along the North fence and ran towards the outside entrance where all of us would-be hawkers would be jockeying for position for the concession manager's attention to be picked that night. The lights were already on and attracting vast swarms of bugs as the players warmed up on the field. The grass was wet with dew, discoloring the brown leather of my well-worn shoes, and I felt my sock getting soaked through a small crack where the leather had become thin on my left shoe. I wouldn't get another pair until Christmas. The players were warming up on the field for the game. The Cyclone fence rattled in front of me as a stray ball hit it, then bounced over the top and rolled across the grass. I stopped long enough to pick up the ball, smiled, and tossed it back to the player that had run after it who thanked me. The smell of popcorn and hot dogs made my stomach growl as I remembered I'd left in so much of a hurry to be on time; I hadn't taken the time to eat. I ignored the pain. I was sure that tonight would be the night the manager would pick me!

Dodgeball

As I walked towards the stadium, I remembered the first night I'd shown up; just one of the many hopefuls hoping to be one of the concession boys that walked the aisles. I know I looked like a fool jumping and dancing around, waving my hands and yelling at the top of my voice, "Pick me! Pick me!" But I didn't care. Instantly that thought brought me back to gym class to a recent dodgeball game at school.

"Okay, guys! Gather around. As you know, the object of Dodgeball is to be the last one standing, so don't let the ball hit you! Pick your teams!" shouted the gym coach to we boys standing around in our dorkie yellow and blue gym unitards. The only place I was the last one standing would be chosen for a team. I'd daydreamed about winning the game. "Ronnie! Ronnie! Ronnie!" I could almost hear them shouting as I took my victory lap within the circle.

"Ronnie!" the Coach yelled. "You're on the blue team! Get the lead out and get in there!"

Startled from my daydream, I'd jumped and run into the center of the ring of snickering boys. I had made up my mind—today would be different. "Hit me! Hit me! I dare you to hit me!" I taunted the yellow team, which snickered at my tall thin frame running around cartoon-like within the circle of strapping middle school boys, some of which would have made two of me. Undaunted, today would be my day!

"Hey, Coach! Are you sure it's okay to hit somebody that wears glasses?" someone jeered, laughing.

Everyone snickered again.

Blake Mansfield, the tall, dark, and handsome star of the basketball team, reared back with the ball, his blonde hair not even mussed from our activity like some iconic Greek statue or something. A few seconds later, as usually happened in Dodgeball, my pale, 119-

pound, rake of a body splattered ungracefully onto the gym floor as the ball hit me square on the side of my face.

"Foul!" I heard the coach yell. "No hitting above the waist!"

This trip to the floor had been different from every other game in that I looked up to see my black horn-rimmed glasses go flying end over end across the floor towards the bleachers to come to rest at the very feet of none other than Melissa Benefield. She was the prettiest girl in school and the head cheerleader who wouldn't give me the time of day if I were on fire. She had looked perfect that day with her long, light brown hair streaming in gentle ringlets down the front of her tight, fuzzy pink sweater. I felt my breath catch as I suddenly became aware that her big brown eyes were focused on me, Ron Meyers. Her beautiful mouth framed perfect teeth as she smiled, deepening twin dimples in her perfect cheeks. I was the center of attention for this beautiful angel and the other four almost as equally lovely cheerleaders, who were all giggling at me. I didn't mind at all; they were laughing at me until I noticed their laughter changed to looks of horror.

I felt something warm dripping down my nose and reached up and touched my face, which had begun to sting a little and drew back a handful of blood where my glasses had cut my face. It's annoying how much a face wound bleeds. The coach had picked me up effortlessly in one motion, quite literally slapping a handkerchief in my face and set me back on my feet in the direction of the nurse's office and pointed to the door. I half-ran out of the gym with the other boy's laughter and catcalls still ringing in my ears.

The Chosen

Another ball made it over the fence, barely missing me and jarring me out of my daydream. This time the player had leaped over it after the baseball.

"Sorry, man!" he called over his shoulder in my direction.

As I made it to the front of the stadium where the other boys were already gathering, this time, I asked, well, more like begged, *Jesus, please help me get picked*. The boys were already gathering around the concession manager. I charged into the herd like a crazy person, leaping impressively high into the air and yelling at the top of my voice, "Pick me!" To my surprise and indescribable delight, I was the first boy picked. Without even thinking, I shouted, "Thank you, Jesus!" I ran to the concession stand to pick up my tray. I felt like I floated across the field as I headed for the stadium where, before my foot ever made it to the first stair, I knew that night, I was going to sell more than anyone else. All night, I walked up and down the stands yelling as loud as I could, "Popcorn! Peanuts! Crackerjacks! Pop here, get your ice-cold pop!" I never felt tired, even after the two-mile hike to get to the stadium. Nor did the heat ever once bother me. I was so full of joy that he chose me that nothing else mattered. Going that extra mile to get what I wanted was finally paying off. I was selling like crazy! Just as I predicted, I brought in more money than anyone else that night and earned my place as a regular.

Almost every time I got home from working in the stands, I felt awesome! I'd stop long enough to wipe my feet at the back door so as not to track anything across the kitchen floor I knew my mom would have cleaned only hours before. The rusty screen door squeaked loudly and banged shut behind me. The bright kitchen with its yellow printed wallpaper and crisp white curtains that hung over the kitchen window would always smell like fresh coffee. Some nights when he wasn't working, Dad would be sitting at the end of the long kitchen table still dressed in the brown uniform he'd worked in that day. His favorite coffee cup would always be there on the kitchen table beside the candle my mother kept lit. (I think it was a Catholic thing.) He'd be leaned back in the metal chair, his back propped against the wall, pretending to look at the sports section of the newspaper, or working a crossword puzzle. Then, he'd look up as if surprised and greet me. I knew on those nights he had been waiting for me.

"Hey, kid, how much money did you make tonight?" he'd ask.

I'd tell him, and then he would ask if he could borrow it. I could never say no to my Dad. How could I? I'd dig into my pocket and hand him the hand full of mixed bills and change I'd earned that night which he'd then shove into his pocket without even counting it, and I'd tell him all about my night. He would intently listen as I relived my journey up and down the stands, appearing to genuinely enjoy my stories. He never did pay me back, but it never bothered me; and strangely, I didn't want him to. For some reason, it just felt right. For a little while, I held all of his attention, and at that moment, that was enough for me.

Henry's Hamburgers

The following summer was drawing near. I discovered that I liked working. It was about more than just the money—it kept my mind busy. When I was working, I wasn't thinking about home, where I worked to stay out of the way of my mother's wrath and disappointment in her 'problem child.' I longed for the day I'd finally be free and had started to save just a little from my odd jobs in anticipation of that day. But, like the usual things that most kids do to try to earn extra money, I got the typical results—not much more than pocket change, and at this rate, it looked hopeless. However, all that changed when I got my first job at fifteen flipping burgers at Henry's Hamburgers. Yes, it sounds corny, but never-the-less, that was the name. I frequented there a lot, buying my friends hamburgers; since, having a strong work ethic even at such an early age, I was known as the kid who always had money.

"Hey, if it isn't Mr. Money Bags!" Al smiled when I came in to get my usual, a hamburger, fries, and a coke. Al was a friendly fellow with a ruddy complexion and a natural smile in his round face. We all enjoyed spending time hanging out there. The diner was immaculately clean; it's chrome details highly polished with the apparent pride Al took in it. The napkin holders were never empty, the catchup bottles and salt and pepper shakers were always kept clean and full, their tops polished just as shiny as the rest of the place. You would never find food on the black and white checkerboard floor of this diner, and the food was always delicious. Susie Bianchi walked past us in her crisp red waitress uniform with her arms full of delicious-looking dishes delicately balanced across her arms and in her hands. She was a cute girl with dark curly hair and a lovely figure that dated one of the jocks on the basketball team. As most guys would, I appreciated the way her hips moved as she headed towards a family sitting at the other end of the diner as if keeping rhythm to the beat of the latest top 50 Pop songs were always playing in the background.

"What'cha know good?" the rather portly fellow asked, wiping his hands on his white apron.

I slid up onto the shiny round red plastic backless seat of the barstool suspended on its silver column and spun around on it a second before answering him. "Not much, Al, just the usual," I smiled. "How about a couple of burgers for my friends and me?"

Al raised his eyes to the corner booth where my three buddies were seated. The idiots were blowing spitballs at one another through straws, laughing hilariously. Of course, this was all for the benefit of several attractive young ladies sitting a few booths away.

He asked, "I noticed every time you're in here; you're always the one paying. Where do you come up with all that money?"

"Well, you know, I have odd jobs. I mow lawns, wash cars, have a paper route—the usual stuff," I answered nonchalantly as I checked out my reflection in the napkin holder.

"How about coming to work for me during summer vacation?" he asked.

I put the napkin holder down and looked at Al, "I'd love to, but I'm only fifteen. I can't get a real job until I turn 16."

"Who told you that?" Al grinned, momentarily stopping to inspect the glass he'd been polishing. "You can work at fifteen. I have an opening here at the diner flipping burgers. It's yours if you want it," he said casually, gesturing in the direction of the grill.

"Wow! Do I!" I jumped up from the stool full of excitement.

"As school is almost over, you can go ahead and start training. You start tomorrow. See you after school, kid," Al smiled as he watched me practically dancing. He turned to the cute waitress and waved her over, "Hey Susie! Come take this man's order!"

After school, I ran to the diner. Once I learned the ropes, I couldn't get enough of it. During the summer, I worked 110 to 120 hours a week for $1.10 an hour. I never left. I'd arrive early to prepare for the breakfast crowd and wouldn't leave until the last saltshaker was polished after we closed. He couldn't chase me out of there; I loved it! I kept all my pay stubs from that first job, from all my jobs, until I lost them in Hurricane Katrina. Al showed me how to use the register and taught me upselling, suggesting larger portions of fries or coke for a few pennies more whenever anyone ordered. I was so good at selling; it wasn't long before I was filling the register, and Al pulled me off the grill and put me on the register permanently.

One afternoon, Al pulled me aside when I was on a break. Al was a man of few words that didn't have something directly to do with work, so when he chose to say something, I never failed to stop whatever I was doing to pay attention. What he said next, I would always remember.

"You know, kid, I've been watching you. Do you know that if you went through life helping and loving people, that one day you could do almost anything? Whether in politics or running a company, people would trust you."

For me, that was a life-defining piece of wisdom. There have been many times since that day that I meditated on the meaning of those words. I wanted to begin my journey in life so I could show my family that I was going to be somebody one day, and most of all, after everything He'd been doing for me, I wanted to make Jesus proud.

Shortly afterward, I became the assistant manager at sixteen. One of the girls he had working there wasn't working out, and one of my first jobs as assistant manager was to fire her.

"Ok, Ronnie, Mary Beth isn't cutting the mustard; so, when she gets here, I want you to let her go," he said matter-of-factly.

It was late afternoon; we had finished everything we had to do after the lunch shift. Al had just finished teaching me how to order supplies and count everything to make sure we got what we ordered once it was delivered. Entirely caught off guard, I looked up from putting away the boxes of napkins we'd just received from the Thursday truck and just looked at him blankly for a moment.

"But, Al, I've never fired anybody before," I stammered.

"You'll do fine, kid. Just let her down easy. Tell her we appreciate her effort, but things aren't working out, and we won't need her after today," he shrugged as if it was no big deal. "You can handle it," he said, slapping me on the shoulder and leaving me to stand there visibly shaken as he headed towards the freezer to pull out some more hamburger to thaw for the dinner shift.

A few minutes later, as if on cue, Mary Beth came through the front door. For a minute, I froze when the short, plain-looking girl with thin and mousey shoulder-length hair held up by a pink plastic barrette smiled at me before coming around the bar to put her purse under the counter.

"Uh, Mary Beth," I began, looking down at her, my voice cracking as I tried unsuccessfully to speak with some kind of authority.

"Yea, what can I do for you, Honey?" she asked, standing up from the counter as she turned and looked up at me briefly through tortoiseshell cat eyeglasses that had little rhinestones in the corners. She was still smiling. She never looked away as she grabbed a napkin out of the napkin holder closest to us on the bar, spit the gum she'd been chewing into it, wadded it up, and threw it in the garbage can behind her. I gulped as I gathered my courage. This particular day, the diner was empty except for staff, so it would be the perfect time to confront her before the dinner crowd started arriving.

"Well, uh, we appreciate what you've done around here, uh, but, uh, we're going to have to let you go," I nearly choked on the words as I stammered, getting them out. I didn't know what to expect. Mary Beth was a sweet girl. Would she get mad? Would she throw things? Would she take off her shoe and try to beat me with it? But none of that happened. Her little green eyes rimmed with thick dark lashes, the only thing that she had going for her, welled up, and I realized it would be only seconds before big tears would spill out and over her pale cheeks. A girl's tears are the most awkward and hard to deal with thing in any guy's life, especially when you're only 16. I tried to feign some dignity and toughness as we stood there silently for a moment with her just staring at me. But the truth was, I was totally at a loss. There had been no argument, no questioning from her, nothing. I wasn't sure what to think. I was used to negative conversations ending in some sort of explosion, but no explosion ever came. She said nothing. It seemed like we stood there for an eternity, neither of us moving or even appearing to breathe. Suddenly, the dead-pan silence shattered with Mary Beth bursting into tears and leaving through the front door of the restaurant. The bells that hung on the door to announce a visitor clanged loudly.

With perfect timing, Al came back from the freezer after setting the box of hamburger on the counter by the grill. He stood in front of me as I turned to face him with my back towards the door.

"Well, kid, how did it go?" he asked.

In my usual cocky way, I blew off her reaction, puffed myself up with pride, and replied, "Well, you know, I gave it to her straight. I just said, 'Mary Beth, you're fired! Get out of here you lazy good for nothing, and don't come back!'" It was about then I'd noticed he had a funny expression on his face. At first, I was confused, then horrified as Mary Beth Pensler came from behind him, her face red with anger and hurt as she threw her apron at me before going around the corner of the bar to get her purse. She never said a word; she didn't have to. The look on her face said everything her words would have if she'd used them.

I never heard the bells on the door, never heard her come in. I was so embarrassed! The apologies gushed through my lips as I tried to say something, anything to let her know how sorry I was, but she was having none of it. This tiny little girl glared at me after picking up her purse again with such fury that I wished she had pulled off her shoe and beat me with it as it would have hurt far less than the anger and pure hatred she aimed at me through those green eyes! I was still stammering my apologies as she shoved open the front door with such force that as the little bells that hung from its corner rattled in protest, one of them fell off and rolled under the stool closest to the bar where we were standing. I looked at Al helplessly for some support. But he just looked at me and shrugged his shoulders, "Hey, kid, you brought this one on yourself!"

And with that, Al walked away back toward the grill. He picked up the large butcher knife off of the counter, tested it by running his thumb over the blade to make sure it was still sharp, then without looking back in my direction, he started cutting up potatoes for French fries. I mindlessly went around the corner and picked up the bell, holding the clapper with my index finger so it wouldn't make a sound. I raised up and just stood there staring through the clear glass of the front door where moments earlier, Mary Beth had stormed out and stared at the empty parking lot as I stewed in my guilt. It was a lesson in humility; I wouldn't soon forget.

Chapter 3
Love Held Me Together

He who does not love does not know God, for God is love.
—1 John 4:8 (NKJV)

Life began changing again, as it often has a way of doing; as I had less and less free time, my old buddies and I drifted apart. However, the day came; my many long hours of working finally paid off. A few weeks after my seventeenth birthday, the school had let out, and I had enough to buy my first car, a 1963 Chevy Biscayne, for $200. It wasn't the flashiest looking car, not by anyone's standards. It was rather like a big blue Kleenex box. It was a two-door with a three-speed stick shift on the steering column. But to me, it was the most beautiful car in the world. As I looked at the bill of sale in my hand with my name printed on it in black ink, I knew I finally held the ultimate ticket to freedom! This bright turquoise metallic machine with matching hubcaps was my answer to finally escape from all the pain and unhappiness I'd known at home! I was ready to live life on my terms now! Within two weeks, I finally left home and moved in with my Grandmother into her upstairs apartment in downtown Cedar Rapids. I cannot express the joy and relief I felt!

Everything I had been missing that I should have gotten from my parents in the ways of affection, approval, and encouragement I got from my loving grandmother. When I was still living at home, my brothers and I often stayed with her on weekends. Everything we couldn't do at home, such as go into the refrigerator, cook, build forts, or hang out in the house—the stuff normal kids get to do—she had let us do. She adored me, and I, her. My grandmother was my hero and the absolute definition of unconditional love. She never held a grudge; though looking back, she had every reason to at times.

Regretfully, being young and stupid, I took advantage of her, and far too often, I took her for granted. I could sass her and disobey her, but she didn't have to get onto me for it. My guilt always overwhelmed me until I told her I was sorry. She would just smile in her gentle way, give me a big hug, kiss my cheek, then tell me in her sweetest voice, "I love you." She taught me what real love is. She also taught me how to cook, iron, sew, and bake. Now, why would a teenage boy need to learn those things at a time in history when almost every young guy would soon have a wife to take care of those needs? I could only come up with that Jesus knew my future.

Gas and a Girl

Speaking of changes, I decided I had gotten just about as much as I would ever get out of the food industry. I liked the people I worked with, and Al had been good to me, but now I was bored. So, I decided to try something new. I found a job pumping gas at a filling station. It wasn't particularly exciting, but it was something different and closer to home.

This particular afternoon, it was viciously cold. It had been snowing off and on for most of the day, so business was slow. The mechanic had already gone home, and without customers, there wasn't much left for me to do. Looking on the bright side, at least with a car, I wouldn't have to walk home. After rearranging oil cans in the window for the 50th time, counting how many times a stoplight changes to green in 10 minutes (It's an average of five by the way) and breathing on the glass to watch the ice crystals form, the telephone rang.

"Clark's Oil and Gas, this is Ron speaking. How may I help you?" I answered robotically, though grateful for the interruption.

"Hello, this is Denise. May I speak with Hank Tow, please?" the sweet, feminine voice on the other side asked.

I suddenly sat up straight in my chair, causing it to scrape loudly on the floor, echoing in the small room. Completely at attention now, I held the cold, black receiver with both hands after throwing down the rag I realized I still had in my hand from cleaning. "I'm sorry Mam, but there's no one here by that name," I answered her in my most professional voice.

"Oh, dear, are you sure? I just spoke to him last month," she replied dismayed.

"Yes, Mam, I'm sure. He used to work here, but he doesn't any longer. I took his place," I volunteered.

"Oh my! I wonder why he didn't tell me. Well, that's okay. I'm so sorry to have bothered you," the young girl replied.

"No, Mam! It's no bother at all! I'm grateful you called! I was going nuts in here all by myself with no one to talk to," I gushed.

"Really? You have to work at the gas station all by yourself on a night like this?" she asked sweetly. That's all it took. She ended up talking to me instead for almost four hours.

"Say, Denise, *The Towering Inferno* is playing at the new Stage 4 movie theatre here in town. Would you like to go tomorrow night?" I'd only known her for a few hours, but I had already decided I wanted to meet this girl in person.

"Well, okay. I guess that would be alright," Denise replied.

"That's great! If you give me your address, I'll pick you up about seven after I get off, and we'll grab a couple of burgers before the show," I replied, trying to quell my excitement and act all cool about it as if I'd been on millions of dates. But to tell the truth, this was my first.

Oddly, she didn't want me to pick her up at her house but at a nearby grocery store. I thought *That's strange, especially in the middle of winter*. But I didn't put too much thought into it, having no experience with girls, I just counted it as part of her mystery.

The Date

That night I took three times longer to get dressed than usual. I must have changed shirts five times, but finally settled on one of two dress shirts I owned, a light blue button-up with pearl snap buttons with a pair of jeans. For all the time it had taken me to decide on the shirt, only the collar would be visible under the sweater I pulled over it. After brushing my teeth and throwing on a little aftershave, I practiced in the mirror of the bathroom over and over how I would greet her, "Well, hello, Denise, my name is Ron. Hi Denise, you look swell!" Then dropping my voice down a few octaves and tossing my shoulder-length hair with my hand like I was a real, worldly stud, "Well, hello pretty lady, where have you been all my life? Hi Babe, get in, let's go for a ride!"

You get the picture. The truth was, in my small rectangular glasses, and still being built more like a rake, tall and thin—I looked more like a blonde John Lennon wanna-be than a stud. Even after all that time, I stood rehearsing in the mirror; I still had no idea what I was going to say when I got there. My grandmother fussed over me, straightened my collar, and gave me advice on how to treat her and what I should say. I don't know that I heard a thing that she said that night, I was so nervous. I looked at my watch. It was time to go! Panicked and rattled and forgetting to kiss my grandmother, I reached around her and grabbed my car keys off the table. Stuttering something meant to be a good-bye, I rushed out of the door, leaving her standing there waving.

"Have fun, and be careful, Ronnie Boy! I love you!" she called after me.

The wind cut right through me as I ran across the yard and dove into my car. It was bitter cold as I fumbled with my key to get it into the ignition. The car roared to life, and a belt squealed in protest as I gripped the icy steering wheel and slammed it into reverse. With the radio blaring Cher's "Gypsies, Tramps, and Thieves," the back wheels spun in the slushy snow as I gave it a little too much gas backing out of the drive praying all the while not to get stuck.

Faithfully, the wheels of my car met the drier street and peeling out in a cloud of exhaust mixing with the bitter cold air; I charged into the night to meet my new girl for the very first time. *Thank goodness, it's not snowing*, I thought to myself as I made my way towards the grocery store. The stars were shining above me, and the roads looked clear. I took that as a good sign. A few minutes later, I rounded the corner, and there she was, right where she said she'd be. She was a vision, standing on the corner in front of the grocery store in a bright red wool coat beneath the streetlight, waving. I prayed she'd like me when she saw me in person. Tall, skinny, and pale, I didn't think I was all that good looking, but I thought I had a lot of game. I pulled up to the curb and got out to open the door for her.

Goodness, she was beautiful! I couldn't believe my luck! I'm not exaggerating when I say Denise looked like a miniature version of "Cher!" I couldn't help but wonder if it had been a coincidence that I'd left as one of Cher's songs just happened to be playing on the radio. She couldn't have been more than 5'3" tall. Her long, straight, shiny hair was waist length and blowing about her in the wind so that she looked like someone straight out of a movie. I parked the car in front of her and stepped into the frigid night air. Joining her on the curb, I offered her my hand to help her into the car as I opened the passenger door.

"Hello, my Lady. I'm Ron Meyers," I said as she took my hand. "Be careful not to slip." *Oh my!* I thought quite pleased with myself, *could I have been any cooler, or what!*

She smiled at me, which just brought more emphasis to her distinct cheekbones set just below the most gorgeous big brown eyes I'd ever seen in my life. To me, she looked like an Indian Princess. I thought to myself again, *how could I get so lucky!* Everything I'd practiced after the initial hello flew right out the window. I honestly don't have any idea what I ended up saying to her once we were in the car or if I said anything at all. One minute, we were on the curb, and the next, she slid across the bench seat next to me, and we were driving towards the movie theatre. My stomach was doing backflips from the confusing excitement as things were going on inside of me I'd never felt before.

Being a talker, this was the first time I ever remembered being at a total loss for words. As we drew closer to the movie theatre, the silence became somewhat awkward, and I'd clumsily complimented her. But now I was just sitting there driving and smiling, trying my best to play it cool, except for the glances I'd sneak to look at her.

What was the matter with me? I'm not shy! Denise thankfully broke the nervous tension by thanking me for inviting her out and telling me how much she looked forward to seeing the movie. She even complimented my car. A few minutes after breaking the ice, we were talking like old friends just like we had on the telephone the night before. I felt it safe to say; we had hit it off.

I asked her out again and then again. We had genuinely had fun when we were together. The conversation was easy and natural. She complimented my usually high-strung nature with her easy-going personality. We had only been seeing each other a few weeks before she became the first person to ever hold my hand and tell me she loved me. As you might have expected, that was it. I was done for, hook, line, and sinker. I would have followed her to the moon and back if that's where she wanted me to go.

One evening, while trying to convince her to let me drop her off at her house, I found out her secret why she hadn't wanted me to pick her up there. I had started to wonder; is she was ashamed of me or what?

"Ron," she began, hiding her face behind her lovely dark hair. "I need to tell you something, but promise you won't get mad and go away."

I looked over at her adoringly, wondering what she could tell me that would ever make me want to go away.

"I'm only fifteen."

Meet the Parents

I was a little surprised at her age, of course, but I was in the throes of love, so I didn't see it as any big deal. I thought it was pretty cool, a 17-year-old high school senior dating a hot freshman. What's not to like about that? "No, Babe," I reassured her, leaning over to pull her hair from her face and kiss her on her beautiful nose, "I am not going anywhere." With that, she gave me her address to take her home.

As it turned out, Denise lived on the southwest side of town, the rough part in the city, mostly made up of blue-collar workers who mainly worked in the food processing plants, in steel fabrication, or electronics. But as I said before, these were my type of people. I was cool with it. I felt more at home in this environment than the nice middle-class neighborhood where I had grown up.

As any gentleman would, when we arrived at her house, I offered to walk her to her door. We held hands and walked up the sidewalk, which parted a small front yard to the door of a little grey wooden shotgun style house. Letting go of her hand, we walked up the creaking wood steps and stood on the unpainted wood porch illuminated by an uncovered yellow lightbulb. As she put her tiny hand on the doorknob, she looked up at me and brushed away a strand of hair the wind had blown in her face and smiled at me. This time, she invited me to come inside and help her break the news to her parents about dating me. Those butterflies came back, but I accepted.

We stepped into the living room, and the first thing I noticed was the smell. Whatever Denise's mother had cooked for dinner that night smelled terrific! I tried to gather it all in, like someone preparing for battle. Not knowing just what I was getting myself into, I made sure I stayed close enough to the door in case I needed to make a quick escape. Their home, though modestly decorated, was neat and spotless. It was evident that her mom loved to cook. She stepped in from the kitchen and stood by the doorway, looking at me without smiling. Denise's mom was just like an older version of her, a little chunkier perhaps, but still as lovely and demure. But her Dad, who had just gotten up from his recliner to take a look at me, was a big, kind of mean-looking fellow that looked like he could break me in half just by saying the word, 'boo!' I swallowed hard as I tried not to appear as nervous as I felt, smiled, extended my hand, and introduced myself. The huge man did not shake my hand that day but continued to stare at me suspiciously. As you might have guessed that night, they were none too thrilled about their daughter dragging me home as both of them inspected me like I was something they'd found crawling around in their garage.

It didn't take too long that they grew to like me, though. And her Dad, whom I at first found so intimidating, turned out to be a really sweet teddy bear of a guy. I think they warmed up to me so quickly because I wasn't like most seventeen-year-olds. Having, for the most part, taken care of myself for so long, I was responsible and respectful, and they could see I was hard working and had ambition. They set rules for their daughter, and I followed them to the letter. As I got to know them, I realized that most of the gruffness he had confronted me with in the beginning was just an act, and it quickly became apparent that her easy-going, friendly nature had come mostly from her Dad. I enjoyed spending time with them, and as I got to know them better, I often shared my dreams for the future of doing something great someday. But, unlike my parents, they never laughed at me; they just listened.

I began spending more and more time with Denise and her family. When I wasn't at work, I was at Denise's house for dinner, and then we'd often go out and go bowling or spend time at the Kozy Inn Bar on First Avenue shooting pool. Taking on the college kids who hung there most of the time was an excellent way to make a little extra money. I could always use the money. So, this night, as I watched Denise stroll into the living room and twirl around in a tight red t-shirt and a pair of hip-huggers with a wide leather belt with silver things around it, Kozy Inn it was.

The Kozy Inn

We walked into the bar of the semi-fine dining establishment, and before heading to the pool tables to check out the action, I handed my girl a couple of quarters. The old jukebox would give you three tunes for fifty cents. I was feeling good, really good. I knew all eyes were on my girl, and they were wondering what she was doing with me. The mixed crowd was of all ages, but what they had in common were that just about all of them were blue-collar workers, mainly from the nearby Quaker Oats and Hormel plants with a few leather-clad bikers sprinkled in for good measure. From somewhere in the back, I heard someone yelling something in Spanish and what sounded like dishes breaking.

The place wreaked of old grease and beer, and the waitress, who was old enough to be my mom, was rather surly, but I ordered us a breaded pork tenderloin and some fries and scoped out the place. I knew I could win back whatever the meal would cost. *Knock Three Times* by Dawn began playing on the Jukebox, followed by Rod Stewart's *Maggie May*, then *Hot Love* by T Rex, before the food arrived. Just as I'd imagined, I'd already set up a couple of hot shots who thought they were big stuff at the pool table, a couple of college fellas from Coe College in lettermen jackets. As I never doubted, I had the money in my pocket to pay the waitress before we left. Denise sidled up next to me, running her hand from my shoulder down my back, and I turned to kiss her. I knew envious eyes were watching. I didn't care. Our relationship was easy and uncomplicated, just the way I liked it.

Welcome to Adulthood

A few months before graduation, I wanted my own space and some privacy, so I moved out of my grandmother's home into a tiny rental trailer for $50 a month, utilities included. It was more of a camper, consisting of a small bedroom with a built-in dresser and kitchenette, a tiny closet, and a bathroom just big enough to turn around in, but the lack of space didn't bother me. It was all mine. Now I was not only the kid with all the money; I was the guy with the bachelor pad and all the beer! I was probably the most popular non-popular kid in high school! It also gave Denise and me a place to go for a little alone time. I was loving this being independent thing!

I finished high school in June of 1975 as a C-average student. Regardless, I was so proud of my diploma! Denise gave me an unexpected present on graduation day; she told me she was pregnant. In my world, if you got a girl pregnant, you married her, period. Knowing I was going to have a family to support and no desires for college anyway, I decided to go into the Navy. I'm not going to lie; I was more than a little nervous finding myself in the middle of more changes than even I was confident I could handle. I loved Denise and wanted to do the right thing, but I was a bundle of nerves; so much so, there were times I thought I was going to crawl right out of my skin! Before I walked into the recruiter's office, I did the only thing that helped when I'd found myself feeling like this. I prayed, "Jesus, I hope I am doing the right thing; please guide me."

So Long Iowa

Putting my hand on the doorknob, I turned it and stepped into the Navy recruiter's office. There, sitting at a big, dark wood desk with a typewriter, a container of pencils, and several stacks of files and papers was a nice-looking slight built young woman in a military uniform; her dark hair pinned in a tight chignon. I wasn't sure of her rank, but she looked important. She greeted me, introducing herself as Miss Bridges as I stepped nervously up to her desk with my hands in my pockets. I didn't know if I should try to shake her hand, salute her, or just what, so I did none of those things. She remained seated, pulling a paper out of the typewriter and looked up at me with some of the most incredible big blue eyes I'd ever seen and smiled briefly. Her eyelashes were so long they touched her eyebrows, which seemed a bit too perfect to be real.

"Good afternoon, Sir, can I help you?" she asked with a slight southern accent.

"Well, yes, mam. I'm looking for the recruiter. I would like to join the Navy," I responded nervously, with my hands still in my pockets.

"That would be Commander Dickson, and I'm sorry, but he's out to lunch. Would you like to come back or for me to have him give you a call? You are welcome to leave your number," she replied professionally.

At that moment, a tall, good looking blonde fellow with a strong chin, dimpled cheeks, and a dark tan with more white teeth in his smile than I'd seen in a Pepsodent toothpaste commercial stepped out of the adjoining office with his hand extended. This guy looked like he should have been in the movies rather than recruiting for the military, strongly resembling a young Kirk Douglas. "Good afternoon, son! I'm Sergeant William Jackson, United States Air Force! Pleased to meet you!"

I shook his hand, which had gripped mine like a steel vice. I wasn't sure what this guy was going to sell me, but if I could get some, I wanted it.

"How about you just come right on in here and let me tell you what we have to offer. You are just the kind of fellow we are looking for!" he said, pushing his door open welcomingly with his left hand. Grinning, he put his big hairy right arm right around my shoulders like I was a long lost relative. His enormous hand held my upper arm like an eagles claw as he ushered me into his office and seated me in one of the twin oak swivel chairs in front of a massive, beautifully carved desk. Behind the desk on each end on flag stands stood the American flag and the flag of the US Air Force. I had just enough time to take in his wall full of plaques and photos before the door shut behind us.

During the three months before I shipped out after joining the United States Air Force, I took the time to get my affairs in order and prepared to leave Iowa, finally. Denise and I had decided we would get married when I came home on Christmas leave. Denise was going to stay with her parents until the baby was born and join me after I am stationed after training. We anticipated our baby to be born in April of the following year. The day I was to leave for Lackland Air Force Base in San Antonio, Texas, was October 19, 1975. That day I took Denise to the movie matinee at the Paramount Theatre to see the rock opera *Tommy*, starring Roger Daltrey of The Who. It would be our last date for a very long time. A lot of changes had taken place with barely even time for adjustment. But we had discussed our plan, and though I was still somewhat nervous, I was feeling pretty good about everything as we drove to the bus station.

But on that particular Sunday afternoon in October, as I stood there somberly at the bus station with my bags at my feet and pregnant wife beside me holding my hand, a large lump I didn't quite understand weighing heavily in my gut. Everything seemed hyper-real. I could smell the fall leaves in the crisp air and was acutely aware of their colors, shapes, and sizes as they blew about the street. Their dance echoed my scattered thoughts. All my life, I wanted nothing more than to get away from this place, to get out of Iowa. I had convinced myself that there had to be more out there than just cornfields, small towns, and this—though picturesque—city where nothing ever happened to me. As we stood there in awkward silence with my mother and grandmother, no one was saying anything.

Out of the blue, my dear grandmother adjusted her glasses and pointed to a particularly beautiful cloud formation in the sky above the river. "Oh look, Ronnie Boy!" she exclaimed, smiling broadly.

The sunlight behind the clouds caused a fantastic contrast of purple, blue, and grey hues. Massive, startling white puffy crowns revealed brilliant silver linings with shafts of light sprayed from them in all directions. The gently flowing river reflected their beauty, so the whole scene was indeed a sight to see. My grandmother was like that. She always noticed the best and the most beautiful in everyone and everything. Regardless of the circumstances or who you were, and she was quick to point it out. I looked across from her at my mother, whose stern face seemed more severely drawn than usual this morning as she puffed on her cigarette and stared into the sky. My Dad and I had been on the outs for some reason I've long forgotten, and had found something else to do; therefore, he hadn't come. But for all the pain and grief I felt my parents had caused me, I suddenly realized I was going to miss them.

The big, silver Greyhound pulled up in front of us; it's air brakes hissing as it rolled to a stop. The smell of diesel exhaust filled my nostrils. The doors of the bus rattled open. Leaving the diesel engine still running, the driver exited and headed quickly toward the luggage compartments of the bus to open them up. Several people who had been waiting with us nearby, now stood waiting for the driver to take their tickets and load their suitcases. I turned and kissed my girl deeply as she slipped her fingers into my belt loops on the back of my jeans, and I felt her warm tears against my cheek. I tried to smile as I pulled away to look in her eyes once more and wiped her tears with my finger. She returned my smile weakly, but I read the uncertainty and worry in her face. I could only imagine what she was thinking and feeling at being left behind, pregnant and alone, as I shipped off to who knows where. I felt a twinge of guilt and regret. I wouldn't even be able to be with her to hold her hand when the baby was born. My heart wrenched as I thought about this, about leaving those beautiful brown eyes that looked up at me with such love and adoration. In those days, I could do no wrong, and I fed on that love like oxygen.

My Grandmother snapped me out of my thoughts once again as she grabbed my face, pulled it to hers, and kissed me hard on my cheek. "I'm going to miss you, my sweet Ronnie Boy!" she smiled and hugged me tightly. "I love you! And don't forget to write to me!"

"I won't. I love you too," I promised, trying to keep together the uncomfortable, choking feeling that was swelling in my throat.

My mother stood patiently waiting for her turn as I let go of my Grandmother to turn to her. I hugged her tightly and whispered in her ear, "I love you, Ma."

She sniffed and managed, "Take care of yourself, son," before letting go of my jacket, which she became suddenly conscious of gripping with white knuckles as I had held her. I looked into her face and saw something in her eyes as she looked up at me that I don't think I ever remembered seeing in her before. Love.

I grabbed my bags, and without looking back, walked to the bus and handed them with my ticket to the driver who stowed the bags in the baggage compartment and I boarded the bus. I didn't want them to see the tears that were threatening to spill down my face if I didn't get on that bus right then. I could see them standing there waving as I took my seat and waved back at them. Fortunately, no one was sitting beside me to see the river of tears that I could no longer contain.

You're in the Air Force Now!

The bus took me to Des Moines, where I joined a large group of other young men where we were inducted and became the property of the United States Air Force. With no party or fanfare at all other than congratulations by the guy who swore us in, we were then quickly herded onto another bus, which brought us to the airport to board the jet to San Antonio. I'd never been up close to anything on wheels that big before! It was the first time I'd ever traveled by air, and though I refused to let anyone else know it, I was terrified. After finding our seats, the stewardess welcomed us and pointed out the "Fasten Your Seatbelt" sign and told us to buckle up. She then went over some brief instructions in case there was any trouble on the flight. The whining of the jet engines had become almost deafening as the turbines began to spin faster and faster. Slowly, the plane started to move away from the terminal and taxi toward the runway. I peered out of the small oval window at all the blinking lights in the darkness and thought about Denise, my grandmother, and my family, acutely aware of a vast emptiness that had grown inside me.

The wheels began to rumble and roared louder and louder against the pavement as the jet picked up speed. I felt my stomach suddenly lurch, and my knuckles turned as white as the plane vibrated. I'm sure my face must have been as white as my knuckles as I felt all the blood rush out of it. My hands had a death grip on the arms of my seat. The only comfort I found was in the fact the guy sitting next to me looked just as scared as I was. Everyone has those moments when the culmination of all your decisions up to a certain point, for good or bad, suddenly hit you; this was mine. For someone who had placed such a high value on the idea of having complete control over their own life, I realized just as the wheels left the runway, that from this point forward, I had no control of what was going to happen to me, and that there was no turning back.

Once at Lackland Air Force base, the lot of us were herded into a building and processed like sheep. And just like sheep, we were shorn. My long blond locks hit the floor just like the hair of everyone else to the right and the left of me; then totally bald, came the poking, prodding and the sticking. My comfortable bell-bottom blue jeans and pullover were history, replaced with the stiff uniform of an Airman Basic. Basic training was impressive. I learned discipline, how to make things shine, and to make a bed so you could bounce a dime on it—in other words, it was a lot like home. Except this 'mother' wore a Smokey The Bear hat and got right in your face to break down your self-esteem. I made some tight bonds with total strangers from all over the country, some with whom I still keep in touch. Looking back on it, the Air Force did help me to grow up, and I consider it one of the best decisions I ever made.

Tattoos Tell No Tales

"Hey Meyers, are you excited about leaving this place and going into San Antonio?" Martin Bennings asked me, shoving his elbow into my side as we held our trays in the cafeteria line to get chow. For some reason, everyone in the Air Force called you by your last name. Our entire flight had been granted a day off base. We were close to finishing basic training, and I guessed it was our reward for making it this far.

"Yeah," I answered as I held my tray up to get a healthy serving of the latest mystery meat poured over a big pile of rice. I thanked the big guy in his white apron on the other side of the counter, but he only grunted without looking as he prepared to serve Martin. I moved on to the vegetables.

"I'm excited! I'm going to get a tattoo of a B-52 right across my chest!" he beamed, swiping his chest for emphasis as Casey McGowan looked over his shoulder, nodding and rolling his eyes. He'd heard that story at least six times already. Martin was kind of short, so just about anyone could nod over his shoulder.

"You betcha! I've already got my taste buds geared up to wrap them around a nice thick, juicy steak!" Casey interjected in his quick Maine accent. He nodded at the man who plopped a helping of spaghetti onto his tray.

"Yeah, beats hanging around this place all weekend," I answered. I was homesick, and getting out would take my mind off of it.

The next afternoon, the entire flight loaded up on a military bus bound for San Antonio. We walked around town, checking out the girls until hunger got the best of us. At Casey's request, we stopped at a rustic-looking restaurant, a steak house called "The Butte Stops Here," which we'd heard had great food. They were supposed to be famous for their steaks and barbequed pork. The restaurant was located across from a massive stockyard beside a set of train tracks where they loaded cattle onto cars to be shipped to processing plants. In excellent spirits, we stepped up onto a wooden sidewalk, which had been built for the benefit of what tourists came through and walked into the place across creaky wood floors. The place was packed! The inside décor was typical Texas, with enormous wagon wheel chandeliers, cowboy paintings, and old rifles, among other wild west paraphernalia you would assume ideal for this part of the country. The smell coming from the kitchen was absolutely incredible! An impressive stuffed buffalo head was on the wall in front of us to the left above the bar. A snarling cougar with two front paws, claws extended, seemed to be leaping at us through the wall to the right, and in the middle was the head of a brown and white spotted cow with the longest horns I'd ever seen in my life! One of my buddies educated me that this was the head of one of the famed Texas Longhorns. I was fascinated! How on earth would they load that thing on a truck! After looking at the prices on the menu after we were seated, I reasoned due to space they must have taken up, it was likely due to the ability they could only fit a few of those things on the truck and had to compensate for the loss of money somewhere.

After we'd placed our order, we thought we would die before they brought us our food. We watched the waitresses walk by, one after the other, with their arms, piled high with plates of big, thick, juicy looking steaks with mounds of garlic mashed potatoes and their famous onion gravy, or thick, hand-cut, seasoned French fries. They also carried plates of long French loaves split and piled high with pulled barbequed pork dripping with a thick, red sauce. We were served wire wicker bowls of large fluffy, buttery yeast rolls on a red and white checkered napkin with honey butter on the side, which was given to every table while they wait. We must have gone through at least four bowls of them while we were waiting for our supper. After one of the best steaks I'd ever eaten, we wandered to a bar within walking distance near the train depot we'd spotted before we'd gotten to the restaurant for a drink and a little pool. Connected to this bar was a tattoo parlor. Naturally, as we were now in the military, the first thing the guys thought we should do after proper anesthetizing at the bar, was to go to the tattoo parlor for tattoos. I watched as my buddies got their tattoos, but I was having none of it.

"Aw, Meyers, what's the deal? You're not afraid of a little needle, are you?" Donnie Cooke asked as the tattoo artist finished up the last inking of a cool looking fighter jet with huge teeth across his right shoulder.

"No, I'm not afraid!" I defended myself emphatically, straightening my glasses. "I just don't want some picture of the word 'Mother' that used to be on my chest sagging into my gut someday! I've seen what those things look like when you get older, that's all." At first nothing, then peals of laughter erupted from all of them; even the artist cracked a smile.

"Okay, okay, you win, Meyers, no tattoo for you!" Martin laughed, slapping me on my back. Several hours, tattoos, and a few more beers later, we went back to base, my skin still as clear as it was the day I was born.

Love Me Say Good-bye

Christmas break, just as I promised, I flew back to Iowa.

"I now pronounce you husband and wife," were the words that shook me into reality as we stood in front of the Priest at the little Lutheran church Denise and her family attended. I asked myself, *is this really happening?* I was only eighteen years old, now I had a sixteen-year-old wife, and we were going to have a baby. I was more than a bit rattled, especially with all the changes that had already happened in my life recently. As I looked at Denise's growing belly, I thought to myself, *Jesus, we need you!* Though I talked to Jesus often, at this point in my life, I never spoke openly about Him or "The Voice" that had spoken to me. I felt sure that would only buy me a ticket to the mental ward or, at the very least, an annulment. No one in my family, not my friends, nor coworkers had ever talked about the church or Jesus outside of the church, not even my new bride, so I didn't see the point in bringing it up.

Even though I still knew very little about Jesus and what a relationship should be with Him, I realized later that even then, He had been watching out for me. Once again, He had intervened in my life, making sure I hadn't joined the Navy, shipped out to sea. Even if I were not able to be there for the birth, at least I would be around to see my child grow up and not out at sea somewhere. With a lack of time and money, everything about the wedding had been simple with only a few friends and family. We didn't even have a honeymoon to speak of as I was saving money to get us a place to live, once I was stationed, and had only come home for a few days. Denise, overjoyed at seeing me, seemed not to mind at all that I couldn't offer her anything fancy. As soon as I had gotten there, it seemed it was time to leave. Once again, I said good-bye to her and my family, finding that going didn't get any easier the second time around.

Biloxi, Mississippi

After basics were over, they had grilled each of us to decide where we would best serve the military. I wanted to go into security, but my eyesight wouldn't allow it. Instead, they sent me to a technical school at Shepherd Air Force Base in Wichita Falls, Texas, where I would undergo training for Hospital Administration. If you've ever watched "M*A*S*H" and remember the character, Radar O'Riley, that would have been me, the hospital ward clerk—glasses and all, though taller and a little better looking, of course. On the last day of training, an older, but formidable-looking man with grey at his temples approached me with his clipboard. I stood at attention.

"Meyers," he said.

"Yes, Sir, Sargent Suarez, Sir," I responded adequately.

"At ease, kid. You're going to Biloxi, Mississippi."

I looked at him, quizzically, "Where the hell is Biloxi, Mississippi?"

"You'll like it," he smiled. "Lots of sunshine, right on the beach, pretty girls."

Chapter 4
Meet Mr. Mom

It's the unexpected that can change a person's destiny!
—Ron Meyers

The next thing I knew, I was getting off another plane, stationed at my permanent duty assignment, Keesler Air Force Base, in a place I'd never even heard of, Biloxi, Mississippi. Just pronouncing, it was strange! Though the word is spelled so that it appears as if it should be pronounced "B-lox-ee," it is pronounced differently, as I found many things in that area are, with the correct pronunciation being, "B-lux-ee." The locals had no qualms about correcting you if you got it wrong. In fact, for some names, you could just toss out every rule you'd ever been taught in the English language altogether. For example, a nearby town's name is pronounced "Wavelund," not "Waveland" as its spelling indicates. And a river by the name of Tchoutabouffa, my attempt at pronouncing it was laughable, to say the least. I was astonished to find it's pronounced "Chu-ta-ka-bluff." The "T" is silent, and there's no "L" in the darn word anywhere, for Pete's sake! How on earth did they come up with that? For a kid who had never been out of Iowa, this was most definitely a whole new ball of wax for me!

Aside from the strange names, I have to say; it was everything the Sargent had said it would be—sprawling white-sand beaches, palm trees, a sparkling ocean, and of course, lots of beautiful girls to be admired. The only place I'd ever seen anything like it was on a postcard. Besides the coastal scenery, there were lots of things to do, the Southern cooking and seafood were fantastic no matter where you chose to eat, and the hospitality couldn't be beat. Yes, I think I was going to like it down here on this little sandbar.

At first, I lived in the barracks, and it didn't take long to discover that we who worked in medical had some privilege on base. No one wanted to piss off those who had control of their medical records or controlled their appointments least bad things happen such as files become mysteriously hard to find. We got to wear our hair a little longer than regulation without anything being said by using Dippity Doo to plaster it above our ears. On leave, without the Dippity Doo and dressed in our civvies, no one would ever guess we were in the military.

On June 1st, I'd put down a deposit on a small, 2nd floor apartment just one block from the beach and once I had things finally "somewhat" situated, Denise and her parents made the trip from Iowa to join me with our brand new, precious little girl, Dawn Marie Meyers. Marie was the middle name of my beloved grandmother. I'm pretty sure Denise was a little less than impressed with the first accommodations I was able to provide. As she started walking up the steps to our new apartment, her attention focused on something ahead of us. She let out a blood-curdling scream and jumped up on the side of the rail and clung to it as if her life depended on it, pointing to something on the step, "What the crap is that!" I looked down to where she pointed just in time to see a giant wood roach almost three inches long run across the step in front of us and fall off onto the ground below. I was glad I was carrying the baby as I believe she was all that had kept me from joining Denise on the rail.

Her dad calmly lifted his sunglasses, taking another look at the ginormous bug on the ground that seemed to be wobbling off toward the grass from the sidewalk below and said rather nonchalantly, "If you have a saddle, you could ride him!"

I rolled my eyes as we all gathered our composure and continued our expedition up the stairs. All I could think of to say was, "Welcome to the South!"

The Storms Come

A year later, along came Ron Junior. As history often has a way of repeating itself, just as it had been when I lived with my own family in Iowa, to the external world, we were the picture of the perfect family. All we needed was the dog, and a white picket fence, and everyone would assume that we would live happily ever after. In truth, our marriage was always a bit rocky, partially because we were so young. We argued consistently, and I admit, it was primarily my fault. I hadn't had much to go on how a healthy relationship should work, and the demons of my past, never exercised, had come back to haunt me such that I became insecure, jealous, critical, and incredibly controlling. In other words, I'd become a real tyrant, impossible for just about anyone to live with.

In truth, I was terrified she'd leave me, so I'm sure I smothered her to the point she felt she couldn't breathe. I had to know every detail of every moment of her life. I wanted to know who she was talking to and where she was going. To make matters worse, I taunted her for having to speak to her "mommy" on the phone every night. Looking back on those years, I knew back then I was an idiot. As most people wouldn't, she didn't know how to deal with all my insecurities and high-strung nature. It wasn't until much later that I understood I was projecting the childhood that I hadn't realized at the time still haunted me onto her. I had given her the same pain and anguish I'd received from others when I was younger. They say you can't love anyone else if you don't love yourself. I knew I still had issues with believing anyone else could love me since my father and I didn't see eye to eye, and I felt my mother had rejected me. I didn't mean to, I didn't want to, but I didn't seem to be able to help myself. It was never physical. But these were demons that would follow me long after she left.

She had gotten enough of it and left me a few times, but she always returned to a pleading husband who gave the same old promises, "I'm sorry! I'll change! We can work this out!" It was drilled in my head by the Catholic church that you do not get a divorce, even if you hate each other. Stay married, or the church will disown you.

THE PROMOTER

The marriage finally came to an end on Friday, Oct 13, 1978. About one in the afternoon, this overwhelming feeling came over me that I needed to go home. That Voice was nudging me again, urging me to leave. Frantic, I probably made over twenty calls to the house, but there was no answer. I didn't know what to do. In the Air Force, it's not like you can just go to your supervisor and say, "Hey, Buddy, I need to leave." So, I went to him with a fictitious story. Knowing my Supervisor was a dog lover, I told him my neighbor just called and said my dog, Sparky, got out of the yard and got hit by a car. Of course, we didn't have a dog, but he didn't know that.

Naturally, he said, "Poor, Sparky, go home and take care of him."

Feeling a little guilty, I barely took the time to say thanks as I ran to my truck. I jumped in the blue stick shift Datson pickup and drove as quickly as I dared onto Hwy 90. The beaches rushed by, the oceans glittering in the distance. It was a deceptively, beautiful day. Seagulls flew high above my windshield as if there wasn't a care in the world. But something inside me told me that something was wrong; terribly wrong. A few minutes later, I drove into the mobile home park and pulled into our driveway. I threw the truck into park and slammed the door behind me as I raced up the steps taking them two at a time. I grabbed the doorknob, expecting it to be locked, but it turned with no resistance in my hand.

"She's gone," I said to myself as I walked into our tiny two-bedroom mobile home we had moved into just before Ron was born. I just knew she was gone. The trailer had an eerie quietness to it. It wasn't just empty—it 'felt' empty. I could sense that her constant threats of leaving for good had finally become a reality. I called her name, but there was no answer. I made a quick run through the house, inspecting every room, but no Denise. Then it suddenly dawned on me to call and check our bank balance, so I ran to the kitchen bar and took the olive-green handset off the hook and dialed the number.

"Keesler Federal, this is Margaret. How may I assist you today?" a pleasant voice answered.

"Good evening Margaret, could you give me my balance, please?" I asked.

"Certainly, Mr. Meyers. One moment, please. Your account balance is negative fifty dollars."

"Would you repeat that, please?" I asked, feeling a sinking feeling in my gut, but it wasn't anything I hadn't expected.

After she repeated the negative balance, I thanked her and told her good-bye. I started to hang up the receiver, but before I completed the task, I froze as I noticed a box of Pampers on the kitchen counter. Reaching out my hand, I had touched it as if to see if it was real and wondered, *why are these here?*

Mindlessly replacing the handset, I walked quickly to the kid's bedroom and looked in their closet and noticed that none of the children's things appeared to be missing. Then I went to the other end of the trailer and inspected our closet and saw that most of Denise's clothes and shoes were gone, as were her things she always left on the dresser. I thought to myself, *that's strange!* I looked around the room, checked the bathroom mirror, in and beside the refrigerator, the answering machine, everywhere I could think of she may have left a note, a message, something. But she had left nothing.

Out of options, I picked up the receiver again, my fingers shaking as everything began to hit me at once, and slowly pushed the buttons on the handset, hoping, praying.

A few seconds later, a woman answered, "Little Flock Daycare, Angela speaking, how may I help you?"

"Good Afternoon, Angela," I fought to keep the stress and anxiety out of my voice as I ran my other hand through my hair nervously. I loved Denise, but my worst fear was that she would take my kids away from me. I knew I could get over losing her, but I didn't think I could survive it if they were gone. Would she have left them? What mother would leave her children? She always took them with her when she'd left before. All sorts of thoughts were running through my head at once. "Hi. This is Ron Meyers. Are my children, Dawn and Ron still there?"

"Hold on a moment, Sir, and I'll go check," she replied.

By now, despite the fact it was cold in the trailer as we'd left the heater turned down before leaving that morning to save money, I was still sweating. It seemed like an eternity went by as I waited there for the daycare worker to come back to the phone. Hunched over the table in the dim light of the kitchen, I mindlessly scribbled on a grocery list that had been left there as I waited. I had been so worried when I came through the door at what I might find; I hadn't even thought to turn on any lights.

"Sir?" another voice came on the line, speaking brightly. "This is Sylvia Saucier; how can I help you?"

"Yes, yes, this is Ron Meyers. I was calling to check to see if my children were there, Ron and Dawn Meyers?"

"Yes, Sir, they are here. Mrs. Meyers left them here this morning and said she would return around five," the woman responded.

"Good! Good! I wasn't sure if she'd get done at the beauty parlor early or not," I lied. Then added not wanting to alarm her that anything was wrong, "I got off early, so I'll be right there in a few minutes to pick them up."

And the Beat Goes On

Turning up the heat before I left the house, feeling relieved, I drove to the daycare and picked up the kids. I walked through the door and announced myself, and a few minutes later, a young woman walked into the room with my baby and Dawn in tow. My little girl's face broke out into a big grin as if the sun had just come out, and little Ron turned his face to see what had excited his big sister. I'd never been so glad to see those little faces!

Dawn let go of the caregiver's hand and ran up to me, flapping a piece of paper in one of her hands and hollered excitedly, "Daddy! Daddy!"

I stooped down to greet her as she slung her little arms around me, paper and all. I kissed her and gave her head a little rub, "Hi Precious! How's my little girl?"

"Look, Daddy!" she said, after letting go of me, holding up the paper she'd had in her hand proudly so I could see her crayon drawing. "I colored for you!"

"Yes, you did!" I responded, taking the paper and telling her how pretty it was. I rubbed her little head again before standing up to receive little Ron from the smiling caregiver. Dawn wrapped herself around one of my legs as baby Ron looked up at me and cooed. I thanked the nursery worker, and after making sure they were snug in their little coats, we headed together to the parking lot. Once at the truck, I hugged each one tightly once more and kissed them with tears stinging my eyes as I put them in the car and strapped them in.

As if on automatic pilot, once we made it back home, after unloading the kids and the diaper bag on to the living room floor, I switched on the TV. Then I went to the sink and made Ron Junior a bottle, filled Dawn's sippy cup with fruit punch, and went back to the living room and handed each to the appropriate child. Emotionally exhausted, I landed on the black pleather couch (plastic leather, in case you're wondering, not particularly comfortable as it stuck to your skin) and just watched them play on the floor. To anyone observing, it would appear as if it were any other day. But this wasn't any other day. I felt numb inside with a strange mixture of shock, relief, and confusion. A rerun of *Bewitched* was playing on the floor console television; an expensive color set I'd surprised Denise with less than a year ago, but I wasn't watching it.

It was dark outside, according to the clock hanging on the wall, around 6:00 p.m. when the phone rang with the call I had been both dreading and expecting. I left the couch and picked up the handset.

"Hello?"

Her familiar voice answered but without the usual sweetness. Instead, when she spoke, her voice was flat and hard, and each of her words stung as if they contained sharp barbs, "Hi Ron, it's Denise. I left with Billy. I just can't take it anymore. He understands me. He's good to me. I'm not coming back."

Though I could tell her clipped speech held back a sea of emotion, she had kept her sentences short, and to the point as if had she said anything more, she might talk herself out of it.

This 'Billy' she spoke of lived in the trailer next door. More like a rutting Billy goat was more like it. He was a pot-smoking drummer who supposedly toured with some band. He looked like a long-haired-hippy-leftover who wore dark glasses most of the time so you couldn't see how blown his eyes were from the drugs. He was taller

THE PROMOTER

than me and built like a surfer crossed with a Neanderthal. Okay, maybe not a Neanderthal. He had long bangs, which he was always brushing or tossing his head to get out of his face. His over coifed sun-streaked hair was feathered on each side, as was the style of the time. It was kept that way with who knows how much hair spray which had failed on the bangs. His perfectly trimmed mustache was usually accompanied by a beard of day-old stubble, and you could smell the Hai Karate long before you saw him.

If he wasn't tanning himself in his cheap metal lounge chair in full view of my wife in a pair of very short, stringy cut-offs, he was finding some other excuse to always be in the yard parading in front of the kitchen window. If he wore a shirt at all, it was usually a tank top or t-shirts with the arms cut out. He'd be barefoot or wore flip flops, and his jeans often had holes in them, some to the point you could see that he wasn't wearing underwear when he'd sit down. He drove an orangish, bronze old Chevy Van, the paint chipping and fading on the hood, and there was rust around the fenders and on the bars that held the spare tire on the back. There were bumper stickers plastered all over the back doors, supposedly from the cities he'd played gigs. The tires that were on the thing looked like they may pop any minute. I couldn't help but wonder; *he's a freaking, broke-ass musician! What the heck does she see in him?*

I was mad, I was hurt, but all I could manage was, "Why? How could you abandon your children?"

"Ron, Billy doesn't make much money. I know I can't take care of them on the road. They're your kids, and you can provide for them better than I can. I can't take the pressure anymore. They'll have a better life with you. For once, I need some fun in my life!"

"Fun! What do you mean you need to have fun? We have fun!" I argued, my jealousy and anger beginning to drown out any hurt I felt.

"You know what I mean," She said, straining to be civil.

My anger got the best of me as those demons rose into full swing, and what I said next doesn't bear worth repeating, but my yelling woke the baby who had fallen asleep in front of the tv, and he began to cry. Dawn crawled over to him and started petting his head.

Involuntarily, tears streamed down my face. I knew she was furious now, and any chance I had of talking her into changing her mind was out the window. By now, Denise had become an expert at pushing my buttons, and she knew just what to say to hurt me the most. This time was no exception as she made sure she strung her arrows well before letting them fly.

"Ron, I took all the money out of the savings account, I know you'll be fine," Denise said, the emotion had left her voice as her words came out a matter of fact. Then she added her poison to the arrow, "By the way, Ron, I never loved you. I only married you because I was pregnant, and I wanted out of Iowa!"

Enraged beyond all sanity, I slammed the phone down onto the receiver. My kids could tell I was upset. I walked over and scooped up my one-year-old son, who was by now pitching a full-blown tantrum. He immediately hushed as I sat down on the couch and held out my arm to two-year-old Dawn to join us. She looked at me, and big tears began to roll down her little face. She hated seeing her Daddy sad. She crawled up on the couch beside us, and I put my arm around her and kissed her small forehead as she snuggled her tiny body as close to me as she could. As we sat there, all crying together, I promised them both, "I love you guys with all my heart, and I swear to you, as long as I live, Daddy will never leave you." So, here is where at twenty-one, I became Mr. Mom.

Still Waters

Once I had the kids fed, washed, changed, and put snug in their beds, I went back to the living room, turned off the tv, and sat down on the couch to absorb what had taken place that evening.

Then I stood up, looked up, and desperately asked, "Jesus, what am I going to do?" I felt that peaceful presence just as I had been aware of it when I was eleven years old when I had sat in the darkness at the bottom of my closet. This time, The Voice said, "Everything will be okay. Today is the first day of the rest of your life, and you will be okay. I am with you and your children."

Strangely, I felt that same hope and calmness wash over me and even felt a bit excited about my future. I had my children, and I had Jesus looking over me. I didn't know what my future held, but I knew who held my future. What started as one of the worst nights of my life turned out to be one of the most beautiful nights of my life. I will never forget Jesus coming into my mobile home that night to comfort me.

I never blamed Denise whatsoever for leaving me, nor did I stay angry with her. Regardless of her reasoning, some people could not comprehend how any woman could leave her children and wondered how I could not possibly be mad at her. I guess a part of me understood her motives, and she knew I would be a good father to them. While true enough, she could not provide for them as I could, I often wondered if maybe that's the part of her that still loved me enough to let them go. But I didn't go into all of that; I simply told them that I believed that Jesus had protected me, which I think with all my heart was the truth. In those days, a man would have never gotten custody of his children, so how could I have stayed mad at her? I had decided that truthfully, I respected her for it because, to me, it showed she thought more of the children than herself. I knew I was in a situation that I had to finish growing up and do it fast. But I made a promise to myself that if she ever did come back, I would never let her back into my life again. If she left us once, she might do it again, and I vowed I was never going to let anyone tear my family apart or hurt me like that ever again.

I'd hear a few well-meaning people say things without realizing I'd overheard them such as, "Poor Ron, he has his hands full, I hope he can do it." Even though I wasn't yet a churchgoer, I knew Jesus was with me, so instead of letting it shake me, I just took it as more motivation to show those people that I am okay and good things are coming. Where my children were concerned, I'm sure I let circumstances both past and present influence me in overcompensating. If it was in my power to get it for them, my two children wanted for nothing.

WWW Brenda

    I spent the next two years in the Air Force, raising my two precious children, and all those skills my sweet Grandmother had taught me had come in handy. She came down to help out between the few live-in housekeepers I went through before I found Brenda. Brenda was a robust country girl with an even bigger heart who could cook like nobody's business. Some of the guys from the base were frequent guests just to sample her cooking. And boy, did she love watching "wrastling" as she called it! She never missed watching World Wide Wrestling when it came on Saturday afternoons. Sometimes when I was outside doing something in the yard, I could hear her yelling at or cheering enthusiastically for her favorite wrestler on the television. You would think they could hear her giving them directions, praising a move, or calling them idiots as the kids squealed with laughter in the background! She'd sling her arms and fuss like it was honestly making a difference, and the more she did this, the more the kids laughed! I never had the heart to tell her it was all scripted. They all had such a good time together. Brenda loved those children as if they were her own. She would read books to them, baked them cookies, and gave them everything I could ever have wanted them to have in motherly love and attention.

Chapter 5

It's Showtime!

"For I know the plans I have for you, declares the LORD, plans for welfare and not for evil, to give you a future and a hope."
—Jeremiah 29:11 (ESV)

While I was in the Air Force, I was that 119-pound weakling kid you used to see in the back of the comic book ad for a gym membership. I had won a gym membership, and the first thing I did was gain 40 pounds. Impressed with the results, I was inspired to sell gym memberships and began winning all the prizes for selling the most memberships. The next thing I knew, I had a part-time job at a Universal Health Spa in Biloxi to earn extra money and began making twice the money I made in the Air Force. When faced with a decision to either re-enlist or get out of the Air Force, it was a difficult decision. I loved the Air Force, and I had a network of buddies that looked out for my children and me. Everyone I knew, including my parents, told me to stay in the Air Force for the children's sake; some even pleaded with me to stay in the service, reasoning that I should put my kids first, not my selfish ambitions. But I didn't look at it that way; I wanted more for my kids and myself. Even after everything that had happened to me, I was still a dreamer, yet determined to make my mark in the world. I believed that Jesus had a plan and a purpose for me that I didn't have to discover, I MUST discover, and I knew in my heart, I wasn't going to find it in the Air Force. So, in June of 1980, I left the Air Force after Jerry, the owner of the Spa, asked me to become the men's manager at the Universal Health Club in Biloxi, Mississippi.

One day while working out, one of my good Air Force buddies, Carmen, from Philadelphia, Pennsylvania, came up to me with a brilliant idea, "Ronnie, your gym needs to bring a bodybuilding show to the coast."

"What?" I laughed, "Do you mean like the contest in that movie that had starred Arnold Schwarzenegger? What was it called? I think the name of it was *Pumping Iron*."

"Yes! That's the one! I mean it, Ronnie, I think it will work! Bodybuilding is becoming a thing!" he said excitedly.

I thought about it for a minute, *what a great idea!*

I couldn't wait to tell Jerry, the owner of Uni-Spa. I found him in his office, working on some paperwork, and presented the idea to him. He laughed, "It's a great idea, Ron, but I could never do that. I got my hands full with what I've got going on here. Things like that cost money, lots of money."

Excited, I bulled ahead, "Do you mind if I do it? I will use my own money. You don't have to put in a cent."

Jerry laughed, put down his pen, and looked at me and asked with skepticism, "What makes you think you can do that? Do you have any idea what it takes to put on a show like that?"

I forged ahead with confidence, "It can't be that difficult, and besides, it will be great publicity for the gym, and I bet I can sell some gym memberships!" I smiled broadly and winked.

He leaned back and laughed, "Okay, Ron, go for it, but I have to tell you I think it's a dumb idea for you to risk money and try such a venture, especially since bodybuilding has never even been on the coast. You have to remember this is Mississippi."

Laughter was a part of my life, both at me and with me. Unfazed, I knew Jesus would help me. And that evening, I talked to Him, confessing that I realized I was just twenty-three years old and had never produced any type of entertainment. And yes, it was true that I did indeed live in Biloxi, Mississippi, where such a thing was unknown. Still, I knew that with Him, all things were possible. Were there enough people here that would support a bodybuilding competition? Honestly? I had absolutely no idea. But I had an unshakable faith I could do it with His help. This pursuit would become my first lesson in walking by faith and not by sight.

I never had any illusions that it would be easy, so I did what I needed to do. I searched for successful promoters who I felt could help me. I never thought I looked at Jesus like a genie in the bottle, though at times, I may have been guilty of it, unintentionally. I do my best to do my part. I always did and still do ask successful people for advice. When I began to call other successful bodybuilding promoters, they were happy to share tips. I learned never to think that you know it all because doing so will most likely lead you to failure. I learned early on to seek out the experts in the area you are interested in and ask questions, lots of questions. Or, better yet, set an appointment to visit with them. I never met an entrepreneur that didn't love to share their life experiences and knowledge. After gathering all this information, I put together everything I had learned, and just like that, I was ready for action! My first event scheduled to take place, The Mr. and Mrs. Gulf Coast Physique Contest, was coming to Biloxi, Mississippi!

A few days before the event, I met with the lighting technician at the Saenger theater, and we discussed the needs. He took me to the stage and then backstage to see the facilities for the contestants. Then he asked me the one detail I'd missed, "Who is going to emcee this event?"

I stepped back, startled, "Wow, I never really thought of that! I guess I will be the emcee; it can't be that difficult!" *I hope* I thought silently. I had never been in theater, let alone emceed any event. Nothing in my life would have led me to such a place. I was the class clown in high school. Did that qualify me for emcee? In my mind, I had decided it did!

Showtime!

That morning started with prejudging, which began in the morning and is nothing but pure business. During this time, the judges evaluated the contestants without an audience to distract them. Some of the points in those days were given during this pre-judging. Then there would be several hours of intermission, and the rest of their points, they earned during the evening show, which would come that evening in front of an audience. I was fascinated with the whole process and watched with the enthusiasm of a kid who was seeing the circus for the first time.

A line of some of the biggest men I'd ever seen in my life stood in a row on the stage facing the judges while scantily clad in tiny bikini bottoms. "Show me your biceps!" commanded the head judge. The men raised their arms with varying degrees of strain and posed with their muscles flexed to the maximum. The string of men responded obediently to more commands sending their bodies into contorted stances. Each of the judges' directions caused whatever muscle that was requested to become a brawny mound. Every one of the contestants had golden tans from bright to deepest dark. Their skin glistened with sweat, and their breathing grew heavier like the snorting of gruff bulls. I will never forget the exotic smells of all the various oils the competitors were rubbing on their bodies to enhance the light. This oiling was an attempt to bring the most attention of their muscle definition to the judge's eye. Their skin seemed strangely paper-thin with every vein showing, so much so you'd think it would burst open with the stress of the strain they asked of it.

Evening came, and I was a bundle of nerves. The curtain was to open at 7:00 p.m. I kept peeking out through the curtains and looking at the growing crowd, while with every second it grew closer for the curtains to part, I could feel my heart beating faster. I was getting more anxious and more nervous by the minute. I was wearing a solid white suit with a red tie and a red rose boutonniere and falling back on my Catholic roots; I speed sent up a few *Our Fathers* in between the production manager repeatedly asking me, "Are you ready? Are you ready?"

I could hardly believe it! Tonight, I was the show organizer, the producer, the promoter, and emcee all rolled into one; more than I even ever dared to hope or dream! And I had absolutely no earthly idea what was going to happen!

THE PROMOTER

7:00 p.m. I stepped onto the stage and up to the podium. I knew that on the other side of the curtains behind which I stood, the lights had been dimmed. I could hear the shuffling of feet had stopped and the crowd hushed as music by Emerson Lake Palmer, *Fanfare for the Common Man* began to pour from the surround sound speakers. I felt my heart pounding in my chest. I looked over at the production manager who was watching me as he stood in the wings. He nodded. *Here we go!* I thought, feeling the same rush of excitement as a kid about to plunge from the highest hill of a roller coaster. The curtains parted; the spotlight popped on, illuminating the pedestal to the applause of the audience. This was it! This was my moment! I leaned towards the microphone, and with a big grin aimed at the full house, I said my first words into a microphone, the first two words which I knew would propel me from that moment on, into my destiny, "It's showtime!"

The crowd erupted into wild cheering as I continued, "Welcome to the first annual Mr. and Ms. Gulf Coast Physique Contest. My name is Ron Meyers."

After that, everything began to fall in place. I will admit that those first few sentences were a bit shaky. But I felt like I'd finally done it! Ultimately, I proved them all wrong. This shy little misfit who was laughed at and ridiculed and labeled a juvenile delinquent was now on the path to do just what he'd set out to do right here, right now, at the Saenger Theater in Biloxi, Mississippi! While the contestants were posing, I was looking over the audience of seven hundred people shouting and screaming. I remember whispering to myself, "This! This is what I want to do with my life! I want to be a promoter!" The show ended with a standing ovation from the audience. Backstage, champagne was flowing, and the party didn't stop until sunrise.

Amazing and thankful to this day, that fear of failure never became a part of the production, I had turned an idea into reality. On May 16th, 1981, I created my identity, "The Promoter." I knew I was finally on my way to making my mark in this world! I believed that there was no doubt that God had his hand in my success. My only regret that night of my final triumph was that my parents hadn't been there to see my first event. The whole time I was putting it together, I kept thinking about them. I wanted to show them; I wasn't so worthless after all.

Page Break

Chapter 6
The Chicago Knockers

I wasn't afraid to fail. Something good always comes out of failure.
—Anne Baxter

The bodybuilding show had been such a success; I decided to go into being a promoter with both feet. I converted my bedroom into my first production office, which consisted of a two-drawer file cabinet with a phone and answering machine sitting on top of it. My new 'office' was located right next to my laundry basket filled with dirty clothes. I recorded my first message on the answering machine, "You have reached the offices of Ron Meyers Productions. Please leave your message, and I will return your call as soon as I can." I thought, with that small start, I was ready now to tackle the world and began to plot what I would do next. I decided to tackle festivals.

Growing up in Iowa, we had numerous festivals within the Catholic Church, which I complained vehemently about having to be a volunteer, but, as I was organizing my first festival, I understood why I was at those festivals; to learn. The ingredients were simple: good food, music, beer, and crafts, so I reasoned, why don't I do that here in Biloxi, Mississippi?

My first festival was the Red Beans and Rice Festival in Biloxi at the Point Cadet Plaza on November 27–28, 1981. The local American Legion cooked the red beans and rice as a fundraiser. It wasn't long I received my very first message on the answering machine from a local Biloxi gentleman who called himself, Mitch Dedeaux a.k.a. "The Purple Flash" and said he was a professional wrestler. His message was, "Ron, you have to bring the Chicago Knockers Female Mud Wrestlers to your festival. People will come. Call me." That's it. Being a typical guy, once he said, "Knockers." I knew that was the group I wanted. After all, what goes better with red beans and rice than girls splashing around in a pool of mud? With my first taste of the limelight, my cockiness had already begun to grow. I was already full of myself just enough that I was about to step into my first taste of what my pride had in store for me.

The Dedeaux Delusion

I sat in my car, waiting to meet with Mitch Dedeaux at the beach in one of the parking areas near Biloxi. About 10 a.m. that morning, a 1981 cream Chrysler LeBaron with a blue half top pulled up behind my car. Out stepped a man with a deep tan, about my height, with a husky build. He appeared to be in his early 40's. He was wearing dark sunglasses, a lot of gold rings on his fingers, and a thick gold chain around his neck. The wind blew the little hair he had combed over his balding head as he smiled at me with one of those small brown cigars that look like brown cigarettes clenched tightly in his teeth. If I'd listened to my conscience, I'd have realized he looked like something that fell out of an old gangster movie, but I was feeling my oats and brushed every flag of apprehension out of my way. I made excuses for him in my head that "he's alright—all celebrities and show people are flamboyant like this."

"Hiya, Ron! I'm Mitch Dedeaux, a.k.a. The Purple Flash! Do you like wrestling? I see you got my message!" he stuck out his meaty hand towards me, which I shook with calm confidence. I wanted him to believe I was one of his type, one of the 'in' people.

"Nice to meet you, Mitch, and yes, as a matter of fact, I do like wrestling! I once had a housekeeper that lived for it," I laughed. "I understand you have a bit of entertainment you can fix me up with for my next show," I grinned back at him, feeling very important and excited to get the deal done.

My excitement grew to the point I could barely contain it as he told me all about the Knocker girls and how close he was to them

THE PROMOTER

and their manager, assuring me that they were the best of friends. I felt confident he was going to fix me up with the best entertainment draw I could ever have hoped for this event. I could almost see the cars pouring into the parking lot and the money piling up. I nodded and listened as he rambled on about some of his wrestling adventures.

"You don't have to worry about a thing, my boy! I'll take care of all the arrangements getting them down here from Chicago and into that mud bath. You provide the pool of mud, and I'll make sure they're in it! I like you, and I know this is one of your first events, and I want to see you succeed, Ron, so here's what I'm going to do. Since they owe me a favor, I'm going to get them down here for you for a very reasonable price of only $1000. And don't worry! You don't have to pay me everything up front! After you sign the contract, you can just write me a check for half, and pay me the other half on the day of the event after you have a good crowd in the stands! Have we got a deal?"

Now super excited to have such a great act to put in my show, I took the extended hand of my new buddy's in mine, which he shook vigorously. "You sure do, Mr. Dedeaux," I replied, grinning and full of confidence in my decision as I took the pen he offered. "Make it happen!" I commanded and feeling amazing; I signed the contract he produced. Setting the pen down, I then, rather than a check, counted out five crisp one-hundred-dollar bills for which he gave me a hand-written receipt. I agreed pay the other $500 on the day of the show before the event when the money started coming in. I felt confident the success of this show was in the bag! He got back into his car, and I waved to him and watched him drive away.

The deal done, I drove back to my office to meet with Dusty, a good friend, and investment partner I'd asked along with a few of my buddies from the health club to help with the festival. Dusty was as solid a guy as you'd ever meet. He was the existential definition of the great American cowboy; tall, rugged, good looking, complete with Stetson and horse ranch. Besides the obvious that drew women to him, he was a genuinely good guy! You've heard of guys who would give you the shirt off their back to help you, well, Dusty was one of those guys. Smart, sensible, and a mountain of a man, he pretty much was the muscle behind my shows, handling all the logistics. Together, we lined up ten different local bands who agreed to perform at the festival. When done, we were confident the ingredients were just right—great food, good music, plenty of beer, flea market booths, and the cherry on top: female mud wrestling! We planned to charge admission of $5 a head, and that would include all the entertainment and a bowl of red beans and rice. It looked like everything had lined up perfectly! I thought to myself, *this is going to be great!*

That Friday after Thanksgiving at Point Cadet in Biloxi, Mississippi, the vendors were set up, the concessions were ready to go, the bands had set up, the weather was beautiful, and the smell of food filled the air! We were as prepared as we were going to be. Naturally, I was the ringmaster of the event, so I went around checking to make sure everything was going according to schedule and that everyone was in their places. I got to admit; I was a little concerned as the parking lot was still empty as we opened the gate around noon, with only two people waiting in line to come in. Throughout the day, festival-goers were just trickling in, a few here and there, meandering about the booths and enjoying the catchy music and good food. I was concerned, but undaunted, I was sure the crowd would come.

Dusty walked up as I was checking to make sure everything was a go with the next band. "Man!" he exclaimed, pushing his hat back off his head and wiping his face with a rag he'd had half stuck in his back pocket. "I'm getting a little worried, Ron. You know, maybe we just didn't time this right. After all, it's the day after Thanksgiving, and most people probably have a refrigerator full of leftovers. There hasn't been enough time to get sick of leftovers yet."

"Yea, but you know that most of those people probably have a house full of kids and relatives and they are dying to get out of the house and escape to somewhere. We're the perfect answer!" I replied, grinning. "Just as soon as it gets closer to time for the main event, they will start pouring in here! Wait and see!"

Mud On My Face

5:00 p.m. As it got closer to time for the mud wrestling event, just as I had predicted, Highway 90 was bumper to bumper with traffic on both sides as the people started coming in. I was fired up! People were filing in through the gate, wandering about, enjoying the bands, checking out the vendors that remained, and concessions were doing very well with lines of people and, of course, the beer was flowing. It still hadn't been the day I'd hoped for, but I was happy to see people coming through the gate.

By 6:15 p.m., the crowd was in good spirits and had started making its way to filling up the bleachers. The spotlights focused on the empty inflatable pool filled with mud, and the air was thick with growing excitement and anticipation to see something that had never occurred down here on the Gulf Coast—beautiful women dressed in scant bikinis wrestling in mud.

Just as he said he would, Mitch had shown up saying he'd arrived a few minutes earlier and had been checking out the festival. He grabbed my hand and shook it, grinning and congratulating me on my festival and the impressive size of the crowd. He told me he just knew I was going to be a big success in this town. I'd wasted no time counting out and handing him the remaining $500 I owed him after thanking him profusely for letting me wait and pay him out of the draw. After tucking it away in his billfold, he stood next to me, chewing on his cigar. He seemed a bit preoccupied, but it didn't sink in at the time there might be a problem.

6:20 p.m. The girls still hadn't shown up, and the bleachers were almost full. Growing a little concerned, I turned to him and asked, "Where are they, Mitch? Shouldn't they have been here by now? We're supposed to start soon!"

"Don't worry; we still got plenty of time! They're on their way," he smiled without looking at me. "I spoke to them this morning, and the manager told me they were on the bus and headed in our direction. It's fine. They probably just got hung up in traffic or something. They'll be here!"

Despite his reassurance, something inside me began to start nagging. Though this was before cell phones, I was pretty sure they could have found a telephone booth they could have used to call us and let us know why they weren't here yet. I chose to fight my doubt. *Still, Mitch said he's spoken with them earlier today, and that everything was a go*, I reasoned with myself. *They are coming from up north, so maybe somewhere along the way, the roads were icy or something.*

6:30 p.m. Not satisfied, I felt my temper beginning to rise as my anxiety grew. I was getting hot, but still trying to maintain control. Mitch had seemed even more restless, but at the time, I hadn't yet put two and two together. I turned to him and said, "You better go call the bus company and see if there was a delay." Seemingly genuine in sharing my concern, he didn't say anything, only smiled slightly, and nodded. I watched him leave heading in the direction of the office, and that nagging started again louder this time.

7:00 p.m. Showtime and there was still no sign of the Knockers. I got this sick feeling in my stomach. I looked out across the parking lot toward the highway, hoping, praying. But, there were no lights coming down the road in our direction. I was an utter nervous wreck. By now, I was pretty convinced I just knew they weren't coming. I sent several of my people to look for Mitch as I tried to think while the crowd grew tense with expectation. I was trying to stay positive, but my anger was increasing to the boiling point, and when I found him, I planned to let him have it with both barrels. Unsurprisingly, Mitch wasn't anywhere to be found. I wasn't sure who I was angrier at, Mitch, or myself for believing him.

7:09 The crowd was getting restless, and I knew I was going to have to do something. I'd have to make an announcement, but what would I say? Worse, what would they do when I told them the Knockers weren't coming? I felt trapped, and despite the chilly night, I was sweating. Everything had suddenly gone so wrong! It wasn't supposed to be like this! I looked up at the bleachers full of expectant faces.

Not knowing what else to do, I gathered my courage and put on my best showman persona and trying my best not to let my disappointment show in my voice, I told them a bald-faced lie.

THE PROMOTER

"Ladies and Gentlemen, may I have your attention, please. I was just informed that the bus that tonight's entertainment was traveling in was delayed because of icy roads. And, unfortunately, the Chicago Knockers will not make it for the performance tonight."

Immediately, there was a loud uproar in the crowd. People were standing up screaming at the top of their lungs, their voices mean and angry, "We want our money back, you crook!"

"Sorry, folks, there are no refunds!" I yelled back over the angry mob. "You paid admission to the festival, and there was no separate ticket for mud wrestling! Unfortunately, I have no control over the entertainment's transportation issues!" I tried my best to calm them with a plausible answer I hoped they see reason with, which was the truth if they had been coming. The fact was, I realized that I had been had and left alone holding the bag. I realized he'd been a pro. He had recognized my lack of experience and played his part to the hilt to get every dime he could get out of me then, waited until the last possible moment to make his exit. I did not doubt if I hadn't told him to call the bus line, that would have been his exit excuse. I had just handed it to him on a silver platter. My pride and reckless enthusiasm had kept me from doing my homework on such simple details, making sure Mitch was who he said he was and for not maintaining control of the situation myself, but instead depending on him. I'd trusted a stranger on face value, and it didn't feel right, realizing I had made such a terrible lapse in judgment. It was a mistake I would never make again.

My answer had not placated the crowd. I began to worry as the crowd now began pouring down the bleachers towards me, and I realized that I was in real danger!

"Where do you live!" Someone demanded.

"Yea, you jerk! Who do you think you are?" someone else yelled.

"When I get my hands on you, I'm getting my money back one way or the other!" another voice shouted.

In fear of my life, I made a break for it toward event security. As I ran up to him, I'd never been so glad to see a cop in my life! I felt relief as the Biloxi Police officer quickly placed himself between me and the crowd with his arms outstretched, baton in hand. "You heard the man!" He said to them sternly, "There are no refunds, and you best leave!" He pointed toward the gates.

The language they used to describe me became a lot harsher, none of it flattering, but they began to turn around and head toward the parking lot back to their cars. If it wasn't for the police, I am sure they would have torn me apart! Disheveled and upset, my confident demeanor had left me. I thanked the officer and slipped around the bleachers toward the office to search for Mitch.

Gone

I burst through the door. A startled Gwen peeked around the corner from one of the side rooms to see what was going on. A nice-looking brunette with a sweet way about her, she was another of my buddies from the gym. She had some bookkeeping experience and had agreed to help. Dusty looked up from where he'd been digging through a box for something in the main room where we had dumped most of what we'd brought we thought we might need for the festival.

"What's the matter?" Gwen asked, looking at me genuinely puzzled as she tried to sum up the anxiety on my face.

"Didn't you hear me on the loudspeaker? Have you seen Mitch? He's gone!" I blurted in one sentence frantically as I swept past Gwen and looked around the corner where the bathroom and lounge were, and finding them empty, I backtracked and pushed open the door across from the room where Gwen had been counting.

"Who's Mitch? What's wrong?" she asked, now genuinely concerned as she stepped out of her office, still holding the handful of one-dollar bills she'd been counting.

"It's okay, Gwen," Dusty smiled at her, then turned his attention to me as I walked back into the main room. "Nope, I haven't seen him since you two were together a little earlier," he replied. "I just came in here to get a piece of wire and some tape. One of the musicians had a problem with his speaker, and I remembered seeing a roll of speaker wire thrown in this box when we packed up."

"He was supposed to have come here to use the phone! I think that crook took my money and the Knockers were never coming, that's what's wrong! I'm about to lose my shirt over that jerk!" I yelled in frustration.

"No one, but Dusty has come in here all afternoon," Gwen chirped helpfully. Dusty motioned for her to go back into her office, out of the line of fire.

"Did you check the parking lot for his car? He was parked by us on the side of the building," Dusty added trying to help as he stuck a small roll of black tape into one pocket, and the roll of wire he'd been looking for in the other. He remained calm, knowing that if he showed how bothered he was about the situation, it would just fuel my explosion.

Without saying anything more, I left the office and ran back the way I had come down the side of the building then turned the corner to where we had all parked behind the office, all the while, hoping none of the angry spectators would notice me in the light. I came to a full stop breathing heavily in front of my car. The spot where Mitch had parked beside me was conspicuously vacant. I was furious! Mitch was gone, and my money with him!

After that night, I never saw or heard from him again. I never went after him for the money. I felt it had been an expensive lesson well worth learning. My first festival had been a miserable failure in which I had lost over $5000. As if this incident had not brought me trouble enough, I had heard the neighbors stormed City Hall and demanded something done about the loud music my event had caused. Even still, after analyzing the entire situation, and thinking about the incredibly low turn-out we had, it didn't stop me from believing that I was still onto something. It invigorated me to try again. I realized I was going to have to make sure I depended on no one else to make certain that where it counted, every "t" was crossed, and every "i" dotted.

Furthermore, I also realized that if I was going to make it in this business, I was going to have to become hardened, move one step ahead, and grow a very thick skin. I'd put a picture of J.R. Ewing, the ruthless oil tycoon from the hit television show *Dallas* on my desk.

I'd imagine myself to be like J.R. and do whatever I had to do to succeed. What I didn't count on was that real life doesn't work out quite like television. I was about to find out as I was about to poke a stick right into a hornet's nest.

Chapter 7
I Need a Miracle

"Be strong and of good courage, do not fear nor be afraid
of them; for the LORD your God, He is the One who
goes with you. He will not leave you nor forsake you."
—Deuteronomy 31:6 (NKJV)

My original title for my next festival was The Blue Grass Festival, in which I planned to have loaded with a variety of local bands who were popular at the time. For this festival, crawfish were an afterthought. After all, what I knew about crawfish was that they looked like little miniature lobsters we would use as bait to catch fish within Morgan Creek back in Iowa when I was a little boy. Some of us would let them attach their claws to our ears like earrings for fun. But considering them food? No way! I remember Granny on the *Beverly Hillbillies*, serving crawfish pie to Jethro, but as for us in Iowa? Not going to happen! We didn't eat bait. I felt very strongly about this. I'd go so far to say that if Jesus had told me as a teenager that I would grow up and produce one of the largest crawfish festivals in Mississippi for over sixteen years with over a hundred thousand pounds of crawfish consumed by festival-goers—I would have probably become an atheist! But, for whatever reason, the locals liked them, they brought in money, so they had become a staple. As the city had other ideas, changing the noise ordinance so that I couldn't bring in the bands, the course of my destiny took a last-minute turn as I swerved to recoup my investment and that's when I realized the humble crawfish and I were about to get a lot better acquainted.

Though the Red Beans and Rice Festival was a flop, I became more determined than ever to make up for that failure. With the new ordinance bringing The Blue Grass Festival to a complete stop, I looked across my desk at J.R.'s photograph, wondering what he would do and came up with another idea. Then it hit me! This Iowa boy made up his mind he was going to produce a crawfish festival! Among other organizations, to get my foot in the door to schmooze with the movers and the shakers on the Gulf Coast, I'd joined the Elks Club a year previously. I'd listened and learned when they spoke about the profitability of their fund-raising events and decided that it was something I needed to get involved in myself. I rented the same facility in Biloxi that I'd had rented for the Red Beans and Rice Festival. Then, I sent out the press releases after changing the name of The Blue Grass Festival that I was to produce to The First Country Crawfish Festival in Biloxi at Point Cadet—precisely one week before the Elks Annual Crawfish Festival in the same location. It didn't take long before I realized that I might not have thought this one all the way through as to the probable consequences of my decision. And as you might expect, all hell broke loose. Unremarkably, I was receiving threats of bodily harm and told many times, "It's not going to happen, you dumbass Yankee!" Also, unremarkably, the Elks Club canceled my membership.

I had a signed contract, and because no one had tried to reason with me as to why this was not a good idea but had instead come at me like a raging bull with its head lowered, my pig-headedness kicked in. I had made up my mind! The Elks Lodge was not going to tell me what I can and can't produce! I stuck to my guns, allowing the hostile back and forth to fuel my fire. Looking back, I believe it stemmed from my childhood, where it seemed I had to fight for everything I wanted. Never taken seriously, it had affected me so profoundly, I would keep on fighting even when it wasn't such a good idea and often end up learning that the hard way. This lesson would be no exception. I wanted to tap into their success by being a week before theirs. After all, that's what J.R. would do. What did I know? I was only twenty-five and utterly naive to the "good ole boy" system in Biloxi. I was about to find out as I took the bull by the horns.

THE PROMOTER

I received a phone call from the mayor of Biloxi. After he introduced himself, he got right to the point, "Mr. Meyers, I understand you are going to do a festival at the International Plaza, and you plan to sell crawfish. I want you to know that if you continue with this festival and sell one ounce of crawfish, I will personally put you in jail."

My response was, "I'm sorry you feel that way, Mr. Mayor, but this is America, and I can do what I want. I have a contract from your city saying I can put on this festival and that's exactly what I intend to do! Therefore, you need to back off." And then, I hung up the phone. It hit me that I'd just hung up the phone on the most influential person in Biloxi. The following week, I received more threats from some of the Elk's members, but still, I stubbornly stood my ground.

During these early days, I was developing an unflattering persona for being hateful and impatient with no remorse, a tyrannical bully, and a con man with a vicious temper. Unfortunately, some of my reputation was well deserved. After being run over so often when I was younger, I thought I'd learned the best way to survive in a dog eat dog world was to bite them before they bit you. Like my hero, J.R. Ewing, I played at life like a man plays chess; outmaneuver your opponent at every turn and do whatever it takes to win. It started as an act, just as Larry Hagman wasn't the man he portrayed in "Dallas." It was a mask I wore to keep anyone from getting close enough to see beyond the front I projected. My latest mental rules I'd etched in my game plans, never let them see your weakness, never show all your cards. I didn't realize the dangerous game I'd begun to play as what was real and what wasn't, started to blur within my soul, nor did I understand how hard it would be, nor how long it would take, to unblur it.

I didn't invest much in relationships outside my own home, and trusted very few people, letting even less of those get too close. I blamed it on my desire for fame and the decisions I had to make in this business, never realizing it had little to do with either, but it ran much deeper than that. I viewed most people as a means to an end. If they couldn't somehow contribute to the bottom line, I had no time or place for them; they were just a waste of my time. I learned to play the host with the best of them, smiling and complimenting even when I couldn't stand the person I'd sit down to eat with. I thought I was an island. I didn't need anybody; after all, or so I thought, the only one you can count on is yourself. I hadn't learned yet that to trust people; you had to be trustworthy. To be loved, you had to be willing to love. That meant allowing yourself to be vulnerable. It was something I struggled with during this time in my life more than any other. So many experiences filled with so much pain and disappointment had taught me to build a wall that I had consciously and unconsciously added mortar to daily, and the mask I wore had grown tight to my skin.

Put Up Your Dukes

Back in Junior High School, when I was fourteen years old, a bully by the name of Gary Peterson made it his life's mission to make my life miserable. I knew the day was coming; I was going to have to stand up to him since I couldn't allow him to push me around forever. The day finally came that we were going to settle the score.

That same day after lunch, while we were standing around in the courtyard behind the cafeteria, he had been letting me have it about my glasses. I'd had all I could stand and threatened to knock his lights out. He'd just laughed, "All right, Meyers, meet me in the vacant lot by the old Johnson place, and we'll settle this once and for all!"

Emery Street was a dead-end street in the old part of town within walking distance of the school with only one house. That house was a massive three-story monstrosity with impressive floor to roof white columns supporting a porch that spanned the breadth of the house. This house once belonged to Mr. and Mrs. Eugene Johnson II. The only thing else down that road were a few old crumbling empty buildings. There was an old feed mill, a feed store, and a small grocery store also owned by the Johnsons. But between this feed mill and the house had stood a very profitable hardware store which Mr. Johnson had owned and operated personally. Being a kind man, and times being what they were, he had extended credit to many.

THE PROMOTER

One night just after closing, the hardware store had burned to the ground, and with it, Mr. Johnson. It had gone up with such fierceness and intensity; it was a miracle that every building on Emery street hadn't caught fire and burned as well. There were a lot of stories surrounding Mr. Johnson's death as to whether it had been an accident, or he had made the right person angry. Mr. Johnson had been a hard-working man, willing to put as much effort into a job as anyone he hired. It wasn't unusual to see him helping at the feed mill working shoulder to shoulder with the men on the loading docks or unloading stock from the delivery truck himself if someone had to be away or was ill. Everyone who knew him said he had been a pleasant and patient man most of the time, compassionate and fair in his dealings, and most people treated him the same way. As I mentioned, there were several who owed him money who lived in the community. Sometimes, those who were on hard times would pay him in labor or bring him a fresh chicken or deer for his table instead of cash, for which he'd always give them credit. But, the one thing he didn't have the patience for was anyone he knew who was able-bodied and could try who wouldn't make any effort in some way to pay his bill. And as there always seems to be at least one rotten apple in the bottom of the apple barrel, Mr. Johnson had a few customers that had taken advantage of him.

One, in particular, a strange fellow by the name of William Plega, had owned a small farm about six miles out of town where he lived with his wife and five kids. Feeling sorry for him, Mr. Johnson had allowed Mr. Plega to charge quite a bit on his ticket after his wife and child had died in childbirth. Mr. Plega had begun to drink after his wife had died, and soon after, a family from out West somewhere had come and taken his other four children away. After that, the rumor was that Mr. Plega lost his mind, drinking even more and had developed a reputation for being very mean. Most people thought that Mr. Johnson had some sort of altercation with William Plega and that Plega was the one who had killed Mr. Johnson and set the store on fire. There was no proof either way and though the police had questioned Mr. Plega, with no evidence, they were to let him go. He had sold his farm and moved away right after that. A few years later, Mrs. Johnson was said to have died from a broken heart. The house, which had fallen into disrepair, had been for sale ever since. They cleared the lot where the hardware store had stood so that there was nothing left but the stories. It was on this lot, where Mr. Johnson had met his end, that I was to meet my nemesis.

After school, we all walked together to the vacant lot, him with his buddies, and I with the morbidly curious onlookers who just wanted to see Gary cream me. Gary was bigger and stronger than I was, and I knew the only way I could win was to catch him by surprise. The other kids made a circle around us with Gary and me in the middle. With the waning afternoon sunlight streaming behind us outlining everything in an orange glow, we approached each other. I folded my glasses and put them in my pocket as he looked down at me smugly. I looked up at him and said, "Now let me get this straight, the rules are…" I never finished my sentence; because catching him off guard, I'd thrown a punch with everything I had in me. Hitting him square in the mouth, I had walloped him so hard, that Gary had fallen backwards to the ground without ever knowing what hit him. I knew it was now or never, so before he could come to his senses, I jumped on top of him and didn't stop swinging until he pleaded for me to stop. Gary never bothered me again, and neither did anyone else for that matter. That day, I felt I had stood up to my fear and put a licking on it.

A Way Out

Eleven years later, I was standing up, come hell or high water, to a group of compelling people. There was no vacant lot or element of surprise. I had no family ties to the coast; I could call for help. And I knew, yes, I knew—I wasn't even in the right. So, I did the only thing I could do. I said, "Jesus, I am in trouble, and I need a miracle."

That afternoon, I received a call from a member of the Health Club, Lester Thompson, the former police chief of Biloxi. He told me in a somber tone, "Ron, you need to move your event to Gulfport. The city will refund your money, and things will settle down."

I knew Jesus was giving me a way out. My response was, "Thank you, Lester, please help me do that. You are an answer to prayer!" Once done, I left Biloxi to head to Gulfport's Rice Pavilion.

Remember how I said I craved publicity? Well, I got it on April 16, 1982, the story was plastered on the front page of the Sun Herald Newspaper. Here is a small excerpt from the article, "CRAWFISH FESTIVAL PROMOTER AT ODDS WITH CITY HALL, ELKS LODGE!"

> "…Tempers are getting hot in Biloxi. Ron Meyers, a local promoter, says he moved a crawfish festival planned for this weekend from Biloxi to Gulfport because Biloxi city authorities protected the 750-member Elks Lodge No. 606 by refusing to let him sell crawfish. Meyers, "It boils down to this," he says. "The Elks run City Hall…"

Attitude Adjustment

My mind-set at this age was: Just because I was asking them how to cook crawfish and how many people attended, they felt I just joined for spying. I just wanted a piece of the crawfish pie, so of course, I was spying!

A reporter came up to me after the Crawfish debacle was over, "Ron Meyers, now that you have been run out of town if you had it to do over again, would you?"

That evil wolf side of me bristled at his words as I thought, *the way he said that was as if they ran me out of town! I wasn't run out of town*! I wanted to smack him one but thought better of it. I looked at the reporter, sizing him up before answering him, "Of course I would! And I'm merely moving the festival so as not to interfere with the Elks festival."

The reporter's expression showed genuine surprise as I grinned at him like I was about to eat his lunch, just daring him to poke at me again. I told myself, when I made up my mind to do something, I go after it. There's nothing wrong with that. Feeling generously diplomatic, I added, "Maybe what I did may not seem right to some people. But honestly, is it any different than a TG&Y moving in next to a K-Mart?"

However, my words rang hollow even in my ears as I defended my real nemesis, my pride, though, at the time, I didn't understand just why. While trying to sift through what had happened, I realized this wasn't really about a crawfish festival war, and that much, I got right. I thought it was about the echoes of my mom telling me, "Look what you got yourself into this time! You aren't good enough." But this time, I showed her! I wasn't a little squirt to be pushed around or smacked! At that particular point in time, I would have charged hell itself with a water pistol to defend myself and my festival. It would be much later before I realized that this was about something much, much deeper.

So, in hindsight, which is usually always 20/20: I knew just enough about Jesus to realize that no matter how thick I tried to build that wall to shut out The Voice along with the rest of the world when I didn't think I needed or wanted them, I'd never be able to build it thick enough. Yet even at my very worst, I knew I didn't want to. I knew I was drowning, but I didn't know how to save myself from what was happening to me, and that part of me was desperately reaching for the hem of His garment. That little light of hope that remembered God taking time for a nobody was warring with the part of me that wanted my way. Up until now, my only thought of God was in the reference of, "If He helps me get what I want, great. Otherwise, I can do it without His help."

In my lack of understanding, I had put God in a box, and if I did break down and ask for His help, I'd usually let Him take it only so far, then grab the wheel back and tell Him with my actions, "Thank God, I'll take it from here." And back in the box, He went. As usually happens when we leave God out of our plans, just as had happened with the Red Beans and Rice Festival, everything went wrong. Had I asked God about Mitch Dedeaux and the Knockers, I undoubtedly would have saved myself a lot of grief and been the richer for it. But as I said, at this point in my life, I hadn't put two and two together. But thankfully, for my sake, in God's infinite love and wisdom, He is patient.

In retrospect, with the Elks, I'd set up J.R. Ewing as my example and not Jesus. The Elks Lodge's annual crawfish festival is an event held to raise money for charity, not for their gain. You can never put your interests before those that serve God; in this case, the poor and the needy, and think that you will win. You will always lose. As for TG&Y, it was a privately held enterprise that didn't determine its new store placement by trying to beat out an event that is raising money for charity. At the time, however, through my J.R. Ewing glasses, I didn't see the flaw in my analogy. God provided me a way out. Though in my ignorance and sin nature at the time, having not surrendered yet to Christ, that part of me that had called on Him and desired to know Him knew it and was grateful for the out—the rest of me wanted South Fork.

My rationale was that my company was new, and if I had run like a scared rabbit, it would have set the tone for my being a pushover. I believed that in confronting the bullies of this world, you must be willing to take a few hits to succeed. While in some situations, this is sound thinking, in this particular instance, not so much. I learned through this that the best way to remedy a tough situation is to go to the table and do it through negotiations. In most respects, this allows both parties to win. I reasoned that if I acted tough on the outside, though inside, I was a scared rabbit; I was establishing the image of a fighter. Even if people completely disagreed with me, in my mind, I reasoned they couldn't call me weak. I didn't realize at the time that all I was doing was putting myself in the shoes of the bully and that sometimes, it takes more courage to admit when you are wrong, apologize, and move on. To this day, I thank God He heard me. He offered a way for it to work out and that I lived long enough to one day understand the lesson.

The Crawfish Festival

On April 17–18, 1982, the Red Sea parted, and I moved into Gulfport without the opposition chasing me. I was now free to unleash my vision for the crawfish festival. Gulfport was a very hospitable host for this event, and I ended up with a much nicer and bigger facility, which was next to one of the largest tourist attractions on the coast, Marine Life. It was like moving from a beanie weenie dinner to a T-Bone steak smorgasbord. I would find out years later, my location at Highway 49 and Highway 90, was one of the busiest intersections in the state of Mississippi. It was a relationship that would lead to my going on to produce over one hundred events at the Rice Pavilion over seventeen years with hundreds of thousands of attendees!

It's said that even bad publicity is good publicity. With the promotion I received, crowds came to the Rice Pavilion to check the festival out, but I think curiosity motivated them as much as the festival itself. I believe many of them just wanted to know who I was. For the main attraction, I contracted a company out of Louisiana, The Right Spice, who advertised they had the "World's Largest Crawfish Pot." It was big! It was on a twenty-four-foot trailer and could boil over five hundred pounds of crawfish at a time. That monstrosity was a powerful attraction for publicity. Pardon the crawfish pun, but it sucked in the people. As you would expect, people were served the usual corn and potatoes with spicy crawfish, and most adults also enjoyed a cold beer.

For entertainment, I added a "bikini" and "best bottoms" contest to ensure a good crowd for Saturday night. I was the emcee that night and noticed that every time I called for an intermission for the judges to review votes, spectators went to refill their beer. *Cha-Ching*! The way everything was turning out, I was beyond pleased with myself! *Here I am,* I was thinking, *twenty-five, single, around hot women, spicy crawfish, cold beer, and money! I just know there is a God as I am in Heaven!*

After the event, men from the Gulf Coast Rescue Mission helped with setup and cleaned up, and I was able to donate $800 to the Rescue Mission. They told me they wouldn't be able to do it in the future with good reason. Most of the men were recovering alcoholics, and putting them in that environment had not been good.

I made a promise to myself when the Gulfport venue became my territory. I was going to build the largest crawfish festival in the state and that my festival was going to be bigger and better than the

THE PROMOTER

Biloxi Festival. I smiled at my picture of J.R. Ewing as he smiled back at me from his picture frame on my desk. I know J.R. wouldn't have taken the way Biloxi treated me without a plan of revenge. My revenge would be a massive success!

When folks asked what I did for a living, I answered with pride, "I'm a promoter!"

The most common response was, "What do you promote?"

I'd smile and answer with complete confidence and without an ounce of shame, "Anything I can sell a ticket to."

Chapter 8

Out of the Frying Pan and Into the Fire

A fool and his money are soon parted!
—Thomas Tusser

My buddies (temporarily) from The Right Spice, who had cooked for the crawfish festival, agreed to come back in July for a new festival, "Good Ole Country Bar-B-Que." July rolled around, the festival organized, and just as they agreed, The Right Spice showed up to take care of the Bar-B-Que. However, when the gates opened, there were no customers. My heart sank. Try walking around an event with the vendors all singing in chorus, "Hey, Ron, where are the customers?"

Inside, I said, "Shut the hell up." I was in a foul mood. But on the outside, I put on my happy promoter face and said, "They're coming, be patient, and have a little faith." I was developing an edge. Determined this was going to work, I didn't want to hear any whiney, negative people.

Rattled, I wondered, *where are all the people?* I had just given them an excellent crawfish festival, and now an encore performance with chicken, ribs, and a wet t-shirt contest! The folks had packed in for the wet t-shirt contest, but for reasons I couldn't begin to understand, they didn't want any barbecue! That weekend, we only sold 350 plates, and Diego, the leader of The Right Spice, was not happy when it came time to pay the tab. I didn't have the money to pay for them.

"I don't know what to say, Diego, I just didn't make the money I was expecting to make to be able to pay you what we agreed on," I told him.

Graciously, Diego replied, "Hey, that's okay, man, I understand. If it helps you out, just pay me $3.25 a plate instead of $3.50. I can live with that." The rest of The Right Spice group nodded in agreement.

I started counting out the money and handed it to the guy who had come up to take it, but when I put the money in his hands, he counted it looked at Diego then back at me and asked me, "You're a bit short, aren't you? You owe us for a total of a thousand plates."

"No, I only owed you for five hundred plates," I corrected him.

"No man, you owe us for one thousand plates, that's what you told us," one of the other The Right Spice partners argued.

Those demons began to rise again as I steeled myself and looked him straight in the eye, "Where's the contract?"

They replied, "We took your word, Ron." Nodding at one another and looking at me like I'd just jumped out of a cake stark naked.

I replied flatly with complete control, "No contract, no proof. I don't have the money, so take what I have or take nothing."

The conversation grew ugly as I realized that these intimidating six-foot-three Cajuns were not going to leave until I paid them. Dusty had been helping some of the guys stack chairs to be picked up from the rental agency and had witnessed the whole thing. I caught the look on his face out of the corner of my eye and knew he must have been wondering, 'Has he lost his cotton-picking mind? What is he thinking?" Taking the hint by his expression that I was about to be killed, I wrote them a check for the additional 500 plates even though they insisted on cash.

The next day, I did the unthinkable. I stopped payment on that check. I never heard from them again until February 7, 1983, when I received a summons that Ron Meyers Productions was about to be sued. The amount was for $1,625 for the other five hundred plates.

Though I may have mentioned I would have paid them for a thousand plates, I wasn't going to put that in writing. In my defense, I genuinely believed after the success of the crawfish festival, we would sell one thousand plates, and I'd have had no trouble handing them the money, had we done just that. I couldn't help but think; *here I go again. I seem to attract trouble!* I didn't fully understand at the time it was because I was supplying the bait.

Even my attorney had said, "Ron, why did you do that without contacting me? It's my job to look out for you. We might lose this in court. Don't ever enter an agreement without me writing it up!"

In my cockiness, I'd shrugged my shoulders.

My Day in Court

My first time in a courtroom was a bit intimidating. However, my attorney, Stephen T. "Tim" Fishel, was a great lawyer. He reassured me over and over not to worry, then leaned towards me like the quarterback in a football huddle, "Ron, no one is going to take advantage of you. We are going to request a trial by jury, and this is what I want you to do…"

Tim prepared me with the expertise of a seasoned professional, and that day in court, he was superb. He walked up in front of the courtroom dressed in his snappiest suit and his shoes carrying a perfect shine. With all eyes on him, Tim worked the jury like a seasoned pro. For you see, if I failed to mention it—this was not only my first case but his as well. He presented me as a nice, clean-cut, single dad who was just trying to follow the American dream but was being bullied by a group of intimidating men. He had instructed me to wear a blue blazer, white shirt, and red tie—the perfect reflection of the patriotic entrepreneurial American. I'd gotten a haircut that morning and made an extra effort to be sure my face was perfectly shaven. I looked over with some satisfaction at my adversaries and thought their lawyers should have prepared them as well on how to dress when they showed up into the courtroom in plaid flannel shirts, blue jeans, wide leather belts, and scuffed work boots. Stage ready. Next to the likes of these, I looked like David versus Goliath as I pitted against these overgrown, brutal-looking characters. Their lawyers grilled me and tried to show the jury I was a con and never intended to pay them. But my lawyer cleverly asked, "Why would you come to Gulfport and cook 1000 plates of Barbecue without a contract? Is this how you do business in Louisiana?"

Finally, the jury came back with their verdict and had decided unanimously in my favor. To my great relief, I did not owe The Right Spice one thin dime. I believe it taught both parties never to go into anything without a signed contract. That night, Tim and I went to a restaurant in Pass Christian called Beezy's and celebrated his first win as a lawyer fresh out of law school. I didn't know that day would be his first and last win for me. Some months later, he would die in a plane crash.

Chapter 9
My Step of Faith

"For we walk by faith, not by sight."
—2 Corinthians 5:7 (NKJV)

I decided to end that year with a Labor Day Festival. I remembered growing up in Iowa in which the Labor Day Telethon with Jerry Lewis was a big deal with events all over the city. So, I thought, *let's do the same thing! We will throw a festival, and I will raise some money for Jerry's kids—I'll make a few bucks for myself, and everyone will be happy. For the draw, of course, I'll have a bikini and best bottoms contest!*

I was turning the Rice Pavilion into a premier location for events. The exit from Marine Life, a popular tourist attraction, was within fifty feet to the back entrance of the pavilion, and people just naturally flowed in. I had two marketing campaigns, "The Coast's Largest Flea Market," for the daytime family crowd and the "Bikinis, Beer and Babes" for the nighttime partiers. What a life! I was making a living for throwing a party! Only in America could I do this. My appetite for more events was steadily increasing. But, they weren't going to happen without beer, bikinis, and the best bottoms on the coast!

Behind the scenes, I had the best crew working for me ever. As I mentioned earlier, Dusty ran the whole logistics, of course. My two kids helped me through their teen years with the concession stand selling cokes and popcorn. My daughter's friend, Jimmy, also chipped in often. A character with a mischievous grin, he was a bundle of boundless energy. Jimmy was all over the place and a tremendous help when I wasn't having to peel him away from flirting with one of the bikini-clad contestants. Albert, a big bear of a man, was paired up with Wilber, who was always smiling. Both were hard workers who enjoyed their jobs, and it showed. Together, the two of them kept the kegs tapped, the cups stocked, and the beer flowing. They helped to make sure that nothing went to waste. I remember an old Jewish guy whom I worked for once getting onto me for throwing away a fresh cup because it was in my way instead of putting it with the rest of the unused plastic cups. I'll never forget what he said, "take care of the pennies, and the dollars will take care of themselves." I paid attention.

At night, Slim would come in. Slim, a tall, quiet black man with a gentle way about him, was my clean up guy. Like a human vacuum cleaner, he would come in at 11 p.m. and work all through the night until 4 a.m. If we needed him to, he'd come between shows. Whenever he'd completed his job, he would leave the grounds looking as if no human being had ever been there. Single-handedly, he would miraculously make sure every scrap of paper was gone and every spilled mess cleaned up. He was a phenom! Then, of course, there was Gwen, my lovely bookkeeper. She collected the money, did the tallies, and made sure it got to the bank. She helped to keep me straight by taking care of all the administrative duties necessary to keep us going. She made sure every bill got paid, and all our licenses kept up. The Police Reserves had become a staple, working all our festivals to keep the peace. I depended on these people for everything!

After this event, I had hit my goal of $3,000 in the bank. It was time to leave the Health Club, move out of my bedroom office, and move into a real office, and set up the business as more than just my part-time gig. I was going full time with Ron Meyers Productions. I agreed with God, "Lord, this is a bit scary, but I believe I can make it." And I set out to find a location. I found an office complex in the Hardy Court Shopping Center in Gulfport, toured it, and found a tiny two-room office for rent for $250 per month.

During the tour, I had the strangest feeling of Déjà vu. Then it hit me! A memory came flooding back from my Air Force days while at Keesler AFB. I had needed a particular type of insurance;

something called an SR-22 because of my less than stellar driving record. The only place I could find that would insure me had been Dairyland Insurance in Gulfport. I had taken a bus to their offices located here, in Hardy Court Shopping Center. *Wow!* I thought, as I suddenly realized where I was! I was in the very same space that had taken care of me when I had nowhere else left to go and was about to be the same space in which I would launch Ron Meyers Productions! Not sure of any significance, but I took it as a God wink as if He was saying, "I know where you have been, and I know where you are going, and I'll take care of you." I still wasn't a real church-going person, but I was learning to trust God. I knew, just as in any growing relationship, there was a lot I still had to learn about Him, but as He had already proven several times how He was with me, I never doubted it.

I found a Holiday Inn remodeling their rooms, so they were selling their old chairs and tables. I bought some of them for almost nothing to furnish the office. The sign for Ron Meyers Productions went up, and I set my new nameplate listing me as President on the desk facing outward prominently and thought how far I'd come. I was like a proud dad with a newborn child. According to all the experts, I was a fool for going out on my own, but I thought to myself, *you are the fools. How is anything going to happen without risk and faith?*

That first Crawfish festival incident had pushed me a little closer to God. It hadn't escaped my attention that even the tiny bit of trust and faith I had when I had asked Him to help me, He had shown up. It had made a considerable impact on my life begun to reflect more often in the decisions I was making. When He spoke to me at age eleven at the bottom of that closet, I believed Him when He told me He had a plan for my life. I had a passion for pursuing my destiny, and I found that passion worked hand and hand with my faith. I didn't care what anyone else thought. I was going to set life on my terms, and that is precisely what I did. I was a single dad, living in low-income housing, and I was stepping out in faith to start my own business. It didn't matter to me whether anyone else understood. I understood it; therefore, I was content with it. And that was all that mattered.

I know by now you are wondering, how can the man who was just in court be the same person that is now professing faith in God as I set up my office? Like children, we grow and learn, many times the hard way. Though I had made room for Jesus, if you hadn't noticed, at this point in my life, I was still professing myself as Captain of my ship and claiming my accomplishments as primarily due to my abilities and intelligence. Fortunately for me, God knew my heart and that I would, one day, yield to Him. But, for now, my main view of God was as any child views a loving parent who watches while their beloved child is discovering their way—to get me out of trouble. Sometimes you have to let the child touch the stove to learn that the eyes are hot and will burn, especially those children who are strong-willed and full of as much fire as I was! So, if I was in the wrong not delivering what I'd promised, why did God allow me to win my case? Quite often, God does things for His purposes for reasons that may have nothing whatsoever to do with us, and thus we may never know in this lifetime what was His reasoning. What you are witnessing as you read this book is not just my inner struggle. This is the war that rages inside of all of us—the age-old battle between good and evil. In every one, whether he or she knows it not, is a war between the natural being and the one who chooses to follow God. Looking back on it, I counted that courtroom win as a lesson in mercy.

On the wall in my office, one of the first things I'd put up on the wall was a picture of Jesus. My daily conversations with him were like a child sitting on Santa's lap with a whole list of wants. I know now that's a common misconception many have of Christ. He is NOT Santa Clause. God's patience with me as He gently drew me to Him is a testament to His incredible patience and everlasting love. He would gently pull me out of some of the messes I managed to get myself into, dust me off, and set me back down on my feet to toddle off once again to learn my next lesson.

Chapter 10
The Power of an Idea

> All the forces in the world are not so powerful
> as an idea whose time has come.
> —Victor Hugo

The 2nd annual crawfish festival was to take place at a time when the mood in America was grim. While watching the news, it hit me. "I Love America" would be just the ticket to be the theme of this year's festival, complete with more than forty red, white, and blue booths plus an I Love America Pep Rally! It was going to be great. Wasting no time, I billed it as the largest in the State of Mississippi. Was it? I don't know, but it wasn't going to stop me from promoting it that way! Since I felt like I was living the American dream, I needed to promote why everyone should love America, the land of opportunity! The "I Love America" pep rally brought several local and state leaders who would give speeches about this beautiful country. The scheduled speakers were State Sen. Bob Usey of Gulfport, State Rep. Dennis Dollar of Gulfport, Gulfport Public Works Commissioner R.C. Randall, Harrison County Sheriff Howard L. Hobbs, and Gulfport Police Chief Larkin Smith.

By now, there had developed a friendly rivalry between The Elks Club and my new company, with each of us trying to out-do the other. I would send a group of my guys to wander through their event, and they would do the same. In the end, it helped us both as both events drew large numbers of participants, driving up the economy of the Gulf Coast. I indeed owed them a debt of gratitude for sending me off to Gulfport, as I lived in Biloxi, my mindset was Biloxi; thus, it never would have dawned on me to go to Gulfport on my own. I was pretty sure the "I Love America" theme would knock our little competition out of the park. I stepped up my game this year with dart tournaments, bikini contests, a kissing booth, a patriotic pep rally, crawfish eating contest, beer drinking contests, crawfish races, and the fantastic Wonder Woman promotion along with door prizes throughout the day.

Regarding the Wonder Woman promotion, one of my former employees at the Health Club I managed was Pam. She was a stunning woman with dark hair, a clear complexion, heart-shaped mouth, and blue eyes with a heart-stopping figure! She was a perfect look-alike for the actress, Linda Carter, who played the lead in the popular television show, Wonder Woman. So, yes, you guessed it, another opportunity for me to make a buck. We found a Wonder Woman costume, and Pam signed autographs and took pictures with the delighted festival attendees. By the way, I closed the kissing booth after only being open a few hours. I had beautiful girls, which was ironically part of the problem. I'm pretty sure that every guy who lived in the woods and most likely had never kissed a girl before in his life had decided to come down to the booth and change his luck. Not that I blamed any of them, but the poor girls were afraid to kiss them! Though it may have been in bad taste, I humored the girls by telling them if we had a dentist booth, we could have made a fortune considering how many of them didn't have teeth!

On the other side of this coin, as we were setting up for the festival, I was visited by several homeless people asking if they could work. Instantly moved with compassion by their stories. I selected a few to give a job to and passed out a festival t-shirt and cap with instructions to wear them. Remembering what happened the last time I'd given the responsibility to the homeless, I made sure to make it clear that no beer drinking would be allowed; anyone caught drinking beer would be immediately terminated. I paid $25 a day and provided meals. To my surprise, these were some of the hardest workers I had ever met. Most had just had some bad luck, and they just needed someone to believe in them. I found out that when I set rules and guidelines, they loved it. They were so appreciative to get work and to feel that someone cared about them and wanted to help. It gave them hope, and hope is a potent ally. I learned a precious lesson that day. Making money is great, but there is nothing more significant than helping and showing the love of Jesus to those who need it the most.

Later I found out that many of those same homeless who had helped me that day had eventually gotten a job, gotten married, and brought their families to some of my events. They would tell their wives, "Ron gave me a chance when no one else would." I didn't realize it at the time, but they were helping me as much as I was helping them. From there, I learned the true meaning of the word "compassion."

A few weeks after the event, I received a special delivery package from Rep. Trent Lott. I opened it at the post office and stood there, surprised and stunned. It was a letter signed by President Ronald Reagan. I still have this hanging on my office wall today. To this day, this letter often inspires me when I feel like quitting, or I question whether an idea will work.

THE PROMOTER

THE WHITE HOUSE
WASHINGTON

April 12, 1983

Dear Trent:

Please extend my greetings and best wishes to all who gather for the 2nd Annual Mississippi Gulf Coast Country Crawfish Festival.

I am pleased to know that the theme of this year's festival is "I Love America." It is refreshing that the purpose of the event is to celebrate what's good about America. We need more citizens with this kind of positive outlook in our country.

Regardless of what we are told, this is a great nation, and we have a great deal to be thankful for. I applaud the patriotism of your constituents, and it is my hope they will all have a wonderful time at the festival.

Again, my very best wishes to your friends and neighbors in Mississippi.

Sincerely,

Ronald Reagan

The Honorable Trent Lott
House of Representatives
Washington, D.C. 20515

Chapter 11
And the Devil Had Dimples

> Temptation is the devil looking through the keyhole.
> Yielding is opening the door and inviting him in.
> —Billy Sunday

Have you heard the Bible story of Samson and Delilah? Samson's downfall was a beautiful woman. During our third annual bodybuilding competition, I met Delilah. Instantly drawn to her, she was a female contestant that caused me to lose my mind. In the early 1980s, there were several wildly popular and quite sensuous movies, "10" and "Bolero," in which the perfect woman in the eyes of most male Americans played the lead—Bo Derek. But even with her animalistic sensuality, Bo Derek paled to the beauty of this young woman. I believed at the time that there was no one alive who could compare to this lady. Delilah Alissa Borgerson was a Scandinavian beauty that needed nothing to enhance her assets. Her parents had moved to the U.S. on business before she was born and never left. Tall, blonde, classy, leggy, intelligent, and witty, her body was firm and slender, but with feminine curves that would drive any average, hot-blooded male completely insane! Any man who looked into her sea blue-green eyes was doomed to be lost. She moved with the grace and comfortable confidence of a big, graceful cat. Her voice was incredibly sexy, sensual, not in a put-on way, but naturally, so that even when she was saying something as benign as "napkin," she commanded your attention.

THE PROMOTER

After the preliminary judging was done by mid-morning, we had several hours to kill before setting up for the evening portion, so I went to the hotel lobby to get a cup of coffee and plan the rest of my day. There she was in the lobby of the hotel, not twenty feet away as we both sat sipping coffee—I at the bar, and her at a table. Her very short white tennis outfit accentuated her tan. A full cascade of loose natural curls plunged over her shoulders, down her back, and dangled just above her waistline like the mane of a lion. She looked up from her coffee and, to my amazement and embarrassment, noticed me gawking at her. But instead of being put off, she held me transfixed in those eyes; eyes the very same color as a wave as the sun shone through it and smiled.

Involuntarily, like someone in a comedy, I looked around to see who the lucky guy could be. Surely it wasn't me! She giggled and crooked her lovely finger motioning me to join her, then to further reassure me, patted the chair next to her at her table. I was utterly overwhelmed that she seemed as equally interested in me as I was in her. I didn't wait for a second invitation and picking up my coffee; I joined her.

"Hello, I'm glad you decided to join me this morning. I'm Delilah Borgerson." she giggled, delighting in my obvious discomfort. I was doing my best trying to look cool and worldly, but this woman seemed to see right through my façade and was quite obviously enjoying every second of it. "I recognized you from the show and thought you might like to get better acquainted."

"Well, good morning to you! Thank you for inviting me!" I grinned sheepishly. "I remember you! It's very nice to meet you. I'm Ron Meyers. You're looking nice this morning. I think you have a good shot at winning," I complimented her.

"Thank you. I'm enjoying the competition and my stay here. I've stayed in a lot of hotels, but The Broadwater has always been one of my favorites. It's stunning," she said, emphasizing her remark with an enthusiastic gesture of her hands. "Tell me a little about yourself, Ron Meyers."

I told her all about myself, about my shows and all about my accomplishments. I was hoping to make myself appear as impressive as possible to this goddess. She listened intently with interest as if I were the most important man on the face of the planet. She was so easy to talk to! She reciprocated by telling me a little about herself and the fact that she was from New Orleans. We sat chit-chatting for almost an hour before she insisted that we go to lunch and continue our conversation. I was genuinely surprised by her forwardness, but she certainly didn't have to twist my arm to talk me into it. I readily agreed, and we left the hotel to eat at one of the local restaurants. After a delicious lunch where we talked more about the show, I told her we'd see each other again at the after-party where we'd toast her victory with champagne. We returned to the hotel in time to prepare for the second half of the show back at the Saenger Theatre. Delilah ended up placing third in her event, and we celebrated with champagne the success of the event and her placing. She told me she was going to be back in town that Wednesday, staying at the same hotel, so I invited her out for dinner and agreed to pick her up at the hotel.

Early that Wednesday evening, I met her in the lobby. She greeted me with a beautiful dimpled smile, stunning in a tight-fitting black dress with a low plunging neckline that showed off her fabulous attributes. I had planned to take her to a well-reputed seafood restaurant not far down the road that was very well known for their excellent food. However, just as we made it to my car, and I was fumbling nervously with my car keys, trying to find the right key, she placed her hand on mine and smiled. What came out of her mouth next was something I thought you'd only hear in the movies and left me speechless, "Let's forget dinner and go back to my hotel room."

Every thought I had of food left as I felt the wind leave my lungs. I thought to myself, *is this happening to me?* Ordinarily, I would play it macho, cool. But, to put it bluntly, I had it so bad at this point in a purely carnal way, I wanted nothing more than to be on top of her like a maggot on a rotten piece of meat! At that point, all sensibility had left me, and I followed her with the enthusiasm of a man dying of thirst promised a tall glass of water. Even had I been following her to my death, at that particular moment, I'd have been following gladly and carried the ax! Yes, as you might imagine, my mind was racing with stupid euphemisms I would never open my mouth to utter, among other things, so I said nothing. I just followed. When we got to the door of her hotel room, she looked at me knowingly, smiled, stuck the key in the door and turned the knob. It opened, and she leaned against it invitingly. I stepped through the door, and she pulled it shut behind us.

From that initial surreal meeting over coffee, I felt a relationship had sprung. I honestly thought I was falling in love, and I was pretty sure she felt the same way about me. She guided me by the hand and had me sit down in one of the chairs by the sliding glass doors of the balcony which she opened, then excused herself to 'slip into something a little more comfortable.' I tried to relax a little as she was changing. The wind blew the curtains, and I could hear the cry of seagulls and the ocean waves as they crashed on the beach just on the other side of the highway and thought to myself, *it just doesn't get any better than this*.

She stepped back into the room dressed in something sheer and lacey that left extraordinarily little to the imagination and smiled at me seductively, staying just out of reach. Slowly, she turned around so that I could get a good look at her. The sea breeze was blowing in her sunlit hair, and her backside was almost completely exposed to me as she turned. My eyes trailed from her tousled curls, which ended just above the small of her back, which drew attention to the little dimples above her hips. As any man would have in that position, I drank in the curvature of her buttocks as one intoxicated. I had been surprised to discover; they were as bronzed as her back. My eyes continued to travel further down over the smooth perfection of her legs. I admired the fullness of her calves, tapering to her delicate ankles. And at that moment, *I wondered, how could I be so fortunate that this goddess would even look at me? Me! Of all, people! What did she see in me?*

She turned around to face me once again, stopping only for a second that I might admire her and smiled sweetly as if totally enjoying my adoration, and softly giggled. Then brushing my cheek with one of her hands, she stepped past me, threw the blanket off the bed, revealing the light sea green hotel sheets. Picking up the top sheet, she lay down so that it draped across her, and she stretched cat-like in pure delight in front of me. I sat there, transfixed. The light green of the sheet magnified the limpid pools of her eyes, which now appeared more of a pale green than blue. I felt as if I might be in a dream as her expression showed her distinct pleasure at my appreciation, her deep dimples on each side of her lovely mouth sank beneath her high cheekbones. The light from the setting sun streaming through the window illuminated her face, causing her eyes to change again, now sparkling like aquamarine jewels. Delilah then sat up, gracefully onto her knees on the edge of the bed. Leaning towards me while holding the sheet next to her breasts, she slipped one of her delicate little feet from beneath her, she struck it towards me playfully, then let it slide slowly down my leg. *Indeed, I was dead, or this must be a dream,* I thought.

She stood and seated herself on the arm of the chair, where I sat, dragging the sheet with her. Her fingers were warm, soft, and supple as she extended a lovely, well-manicured finger to trace my lips, then my ear. Then, she bent to kiss me lightly, teasing at first, tugging on my bottom lip gently, playfully with her perfect teeth. Sensuously, she dropped the sheet ever so slightly, just enough as if to remind me what she concealed beneath it as if I could forget. I drank in her fragrance, which by now was so far into my head, I could barely think straight. I felt my own heart pounding in my eardrums as it was beating so fast, I thought it would explode.

"You know, I've been thinking," she said. Her voice held a lyrical melodic tone about it that had my stomach full of butterflies.

"Um?" I managed to giggle like a schoolboy, closing my eyes, totally enjoying her seduction.

"I think there's a lot of potential in Ron Meyers Productions," she said softly then let her tongue trace the rim of my ear.

I opened one of my eyes, then the other, and stared at points above us on the popcorn ceiling, waiting for her next words as I grew suddenly strangely uneasy. I didn't move; I didn't breathe as the dream began to splinter. As badly as I wanted to believe she liked me, I hadn't been able to shake this feeling that there was a reason this woman who could have anyone in the world, suddenly wanted me. Something told me I was about to find out why, and the intoxication

THE PROMOTER

I had felt only moments before began to dissolve into heartbreaking sobriety.

She let the sheet drop as she stood and ran her fingers through my hair, down my arm, and to my hand. But I didn't loosen my grip on the arm of the chair at her invitation. Her spell had shattered, and I felt a coldness wash over me. Something inside of me knew the words coming even before they fell from her lips. She was about to cross the boundary into the only thing I loved more than I could love any woman, and the single territory I could never share. There was no room but for one set of hands-on the reins of building my company—mine.

"I think we would make a wonderful team together," she purred, her words spilling from her mouth like liquid silver as she played with my hair with the delicate little finger of her other hand as she leaned into me. "I'd like to take over the management, run the shows for you, and help you go big time."

I swear I could almost audibly hear this beautiful dream crack, shatter, and fall tinkling to the floor in millions of tiny pieces. The evening light of the setting sun that had only moments before bathed the room in this amazingly surreal light had suddenly faded and seemed to lose its magic. And, the place became just another hotel room, the day, just another day. There would be no building it back from this, not even for her.

Completely sober now, I turned in the chair to face her, "That ain't happening, Babe. It's my company, and no matter how beautiful you are…" I smiled, letting the sentence trail off as I lifted her chin so that she would look at me again since she had dropped her eyes at the intensity of my gaze. She knew they no longer smoldered with desire for her, but with something else she hadn't expected, and I could tell it frightened her. "…and you are beautiful," I continued wistfully, then more firmly. "But I am in charge, and only my vision for it is what I am interested in."

She got up without a word as I watched her dress. Without so much as a good-bye, she left the room, shutting the door behind her. That was the very last time I saw her. I never heard from her again. She was so beautiful, so incredibly beautiful; but, something somewhere deep in my gut was rippling with warnings shouting, "Trouble!" Up until that point, I'd pushed it aside, actually drinking the excitement of this dangerous woman. If that still small voice I attributed to God had not warned me, there is a high probability that I would have given her control of the company, the company I built, and which I wasn't going to share with anybody. I may have had some big cracks in my character back in those days, but I still had some scruples. Samson may have lost his head and thus his hair to his Delilah, but I wasn't letting this Delilah anywhere near me with her scissors!

The Invisible Fish

A few months later, I brought a new event to Gulfport, The Gumbo Festival. I needed an attention-getting promotion. This time, I found an aquarium, filled it with water, and all the goodies to make it look spectacular, everything but fish. That's right, no fish. I put up a sign that said, "Come see the amazing invisible fish from the Amazon rainforest." It wasn't long before a small crowd began to gather around the tank. Customers would just stand and stare; some would yell, "There isn't any fish in there!"

Others would yell, "Yes, there is! You can see the water move!"

The water moved because things in the air fell in the water, mainly bugs. That year, I understood the words of P.T. Barnum, "There's a sucker born every minute." There never was any fish, but none-the-less, people would stand there and stare at nothing. I was curious to see how people would react to my gimmick. But unless they are reading this book, they never did discover the hoax.

After the event was over, I told my associates, "There are some gullible people in this world." It was a lesson for me in human psychology. As I discovered, people do want to believe in the impossible, and if they don't learn to listen to that still small voice, they could very well fall into the trap of deception.

Chapter 12

The Monster Arm Wrestling Machine

> The key to realizing a dream is to focus not on
> success but on significance—and then
> even the small steps and little victories along
> your path will take on greater meaning.
> —Oprah Winfrey

Things got a little tight, and I needed a revenue stream for November to March—something indoors. I saw this advertisement in Entrepreneur Magazine about buying a franchise for The Monster Arm Wrestling Machine. As the headquarters was in Des Moines, Iowa, not far from where I grew up, I decided to make the arduous trip back to my home state to check it out. Graciously greeted by their representatives, they wasted no time ushering me into their showroom, where I took my first look at the thing. The monstrosity consisted of a handlebar apparatus, much like a pair of bicycle handlebars, suspended over a table, with each player attempting to wrestle their side of the handlebar to the lowest point, which would cause the winner's side to light up. A referee was on hand to ensure proper use. It brought a sort of scientific approach to an age-old sport. There was no way to cheat the thing, and you didn't have to worry about the grip on your opponent because you didn't touch anything but the handlebar. My mind started racing. I knew this was going to be a hit. The next thing you know, I purchased the rights for the State of Mississippi and was loading it into the back of my truck and headed back South. I couldn't wait to show this to the team!

The machine would make its debut promoted as the Mississippi Monster Arm Wrestling Machine at Papa's Honky Tonk in Biloxi. To our delight, "The Monster" was a great success! It was featured in arm wrestling tournaments at the coast nightspots, eventually leading to a regional competition, a state event, and a national championship. We charged a $5 entry fee for double-elimination tournaments. In no time, we were all over the coast! They even booked The Monster at the Navy Base in Gulfport and the Keesler Airman's Club in Biloxi. Soon we had an array of merchandising material ranging from gloves to towels to men's and women's underwear to promote "The Monster." The men's underwear had the phrase, "Have you seen my Monster," and the lady's undies had printed on them, "Home of the Monster." We were selling them like hotcakes, and the money was rolling in! The competitors loved them! Looking back, I often wonder if I warped my kids' view of life with this somewhat twisted sense of humor.

Stroh's beer sponsored The Monster nationwide, including Mississippi. We split it up into five weight divisions ranging from flyweight to super heavyweight. The Monster became a welcome addition to all of our festivals from then on. The tournaments continued for over three years. It was retired after a contestant snapped a bone in his arm. It was a great run, but when the liability problem became an issue, I never touched the machine again after that incident.

My promotions were getting publicity with stories in the entertainment section of the local newspaper, and the attention I had sought so desperately as a young person was continuing to grow exponentially. But it was just attention. Financially, I was struggling. I knew that soon I was going to have to make a tough decision—should I keep pursuing this dream, or should I hang it up?

Chapter 13
The Death of My Lawyer

It's the things you least expect that hit you the hardest.
—Ron Meyers

Friday evening, December 2, 1983, I was at the Rice Pavilion in Gulfport, marking off the pavement with chalk for the Christmas Market the next day. It was a very eerie evening as the fog was so thick you couldn't see five feet in front of you. When we left the pavilion, I told Dusty, "Let's finish this in the morning. Be careful driving home. It's dangerous out there." I had an eerie feeling about that night.

The next day, about ten o'clock in the morning, while in the concession stand, I was serving coffee to a customer when a friend of mine, George O'Connor, came to the pavilion and said he needed to tell me something before I heard it on the news. I could tell whatever story he had; it wasn't good news.

"Hey buddy, I'm sorry. But our friend Tim was killed in a plane crash last night. He had initially escaped the plane, but he had gone back in to try and save his Uncle. He never made it back out."

I just stared at George for a moment and leaned against the wall for support as I suddenly felt sick to my stomach. Tim, if you'll remember, had been my good friend and lawyer that had gotten me out of a jam not too long ago with The Right Spice. He had just finished law school at Ole Miss. I'd met Tim while working at the Health Club. I was utterly devastated. Tim had always encouraged me to pursue my dreams. He pushed me to move past the negativity.

He taught me to look at the many problems that came with trying to start a business—not as obstacles—but as a challenge to be conquered. He had understood that I was a dreamer, and I could still hear him telling me, "Ron, I believe in you, and I want to be part of whatever you do." It seemed like a bad dream. I just couldn't believe he was gone! I remembered our celebrating after the court win. I can still see it so clearly in my mind; the room, the food, the drinks, the laughter, and, most of all, the love of real friends. I went through the rest of the day kind of numb and dazed.

By midday, one of the exhibitors came up to me and said, "Ron, you are outgrowing this pavilion. Have you ever considered moving your Christmas event into the coliseum?"

My first thought was, *Tim, are you sending me a message from heaven?* The exhibitor had planted a seed in my head, and over the next few weeks, I wondered if maybe I should seriously consider his suggestion. I had thought about quitting. It hadn't been a very successful year, and now with the loss of my dear friend, I had thoughts of, "What the hell am I doing?" Realistically, I was barely getting by financially. Though one side of me enjoyed selling beer and promoting bikinis to make a living, the other side of me had begun to war with that enjoyment, even thinking that it was cheap and gimmicky. Things had gotten so bad that Christmas that I had to sell my piano so I could buy a few Christmas gifts for Dawn and Ron. I had just about convinced myself it was time to give up and throw in the towel. I was stressed out and tired. Not knowing what else to do or where else to turn, I'd even considered moving to Atlanta for work. I had also begun to doubt my newly deepened faith and wondered, *Am I just an idiot to believe that God cares about me? If so, why am I struggling so much to get by?* After all, I still wasn't exactly accepted in the community either, convinced it was my northern accent that had people saying things like, "He's just a shyster promoter; don't trust him."

One afternoon after I'd finished working out at the gym, I'd sat down to rest on a nearby piece of exercise equipment. I found myself staring at the bench against the wall by the window just to my left where Tim and I would always hang out and discuss whatever had been going on in our lives at the time. Our conversations had usually centered around work or girls we were seeing, nothing particularly deep—just two good friends hanging out together, blowing off some steam and enjoying life. I was alone in the room and found myself talking to the empty bench, "Tim, I don't know if I can do this anymore. I need my friend to help me, and now I am all alone."

I put on this act in public, but deep down, I am afraid for myself, and most of all, for my children. My mom's words were getting louder. I was ready to accept that she might have been right. Maybe it was true. Perhaps I wasn't cut out for this type of life.

Even while this war was going on inside of me, I still felt that God was up to something. It wasn't very long afterward; I had been sitting at my desk and heard that voice again; The Voice, urging me to pursue the exhibitor's suggestion of doing a Christmas Craft Show in the Coliseum. It dawned on me that it took as much work to put a small event together as it would a big event. The only difference was the initial investment. I decided to focus on producing three large events a year and only do the more successful smaller events to keep revenue coming in. The smaller events were also vehicles to promote more significant events. That would be the direction for next year, and if that didn't work, then I would have no choice but to find what others called "a real job."

I still believe that God had me on His potter's wheel. He just couldn't get me to sit still long enough to be shaped into the person I needed to become. While writing this book, my youngest son, Jacob, was attending Ole Miss. I went to visit him, and as I was walking along the sidewalks beneath the enormous oaks on campus, I couldn't help but wonder if I was walking along on the very same path, my dear friend, Stephen Timothy Fishel had walked when he had attended there.

Chapter 14
Music and Merry Christmas

New information makes new and fresh ideas possible.
—Zig Ziglar

Since I had decided not to move away, I started working on my plan for 1984. I needed some sound equipment for the smaller events, so I contacted my friend Alan, whom I was paying to provide sound at my shows, and asked him if he could give me a package deal. He told me that as often as I needed it, I probably should buy a sound system.

That's not a bad idea, I thought. *If I buy it, it will pay for itself, and most of all, I wouldn't have to depend on Alan anymore.* Don't get me wrong, I liked Alan, but he was in the Air Force and only temporarily assigned to Keesler Air Force Base. I knew he could be called away at any time, and I'd be stuck at ground zero again, looking for someone to fill his place. After thanking him, I told him I was going to think about it and that I'd get back to him. A few days later, not being the type to usually just jump into anything, I'd given the matter considerable thought and realized my initial thoughts on the matter had been right. Buying the equipment was the way to go. And then I got another idea! I could become a DJ as a side gig and earn the extra income I needed that way. The first thing I had to do was get my hands on $1,000 to buy equipment, so I went to bank after bank, but each turned me down for a loan. My last stop was Magnolia Federal Credit Union in Hardy Court Shopping Center. The branch manager was kind and understanding. She gave me a credit line of $1,000, exactly what I needed. The next stop was Radio Shack for two turntables, a microphone, receiver, and speakers. DJ Ron was ready for hire!

I hired myself out on weekends at parties, weddings, and, of course, at my events. By becoming a DJ, it also gave me the ability to see how people responded to music. I thought it was pretty cool how I could control the dance floor with music, and I enjoyed how the slow songs brought the love birds onto the floor. I was learning a lot that thirty years from now would benefit me when I became a DJ at a Christian Radio Station. But I'm getting ahead of myself. Wait. What? Are you laughing? It's alright. In those days, I would have been too. If someone told me then that I would one day be in Christian Radio, I would have asked them if they would mind sharing that pot they'd been smoking!

Christmas Fair and Craft Sale Comes to Biloxi Coliseum

In pursuing the idea of moving the Christmas Market into the Coliseum in Biloxi, I needed the perfect date for a Christmas event. It was time for some research. The question I had to answer was, when do people have the most money at Christmas time? I called as many banks as I could and asked them when they mailed out Christmas club checks, and the most common answer was the first week of November. So, I settled on the second Saturday in November. The inaugural event was November 10, 1984. The official name would be "Christmas Arts and Crafts Fair." Giving in to temptation once again, I asked if I could sell beer, to which they responded with an emphatic "no." Aramark controlled concessions in the Coliseum. An event without beer; that was going to be a novel approach. Could I even make money without beer? Honestly, I was skeptical, but I had made up my mind I was going to find out.

The Rice Pavilion Christmas Market had featured Christmas items, but on a much smaller scale with only fifty booths of arts and crafts. However, since I had a loyal following in Gulfport, I decided I would still do the Christmas Market in Gulfport this year. I'd use it for marketing my new event, which would be the following week inside the Mississippi Coast Coliseum. It was one thing drawing hundreds of shoppers at the Rice Pavilion amongst fifty booths, but I knew I would need thousands of shoppers to come to the Coliseum. I planned to eliminate the Christmas Market at the Rice Pavilion the following year if I could create a successful event in Biloxi. So, my career in the event business was about to come full circle. I started in Biloxi, and now, years later, I was going back to Biloxi and bringing a show that would be bigger than ever.

People in South Mississippi love the word "Free." It doesn't matter what you're giving away, if it's free, you can expect droves of people to show up to get it. So, in a one-inch by a one-inch newspaper ad, I advertised the latest extravaganza to feature a plethora of free giveaways. Free parking, free admission, free Pepsi, free coffee, free arcade games, and finally, free big fat Thanksgiving turkeys were to be given away hourly. I was pretty sure the word "free" would attract thousands of customers, and it surely did! The Christmas Craft Sale featured 130 booths of Christmas gifts and items of all shapes, sizes, styles, colors, and varieties. From fine porcelain to handcrafted items, quilts, macramé, dolls, and a bit of everything else you could think of to satisfy all tastes were available for purchase. And, of course, Santa Clause came fresh from a North Pole trip for photographs in a lovely souvenir folder for $5.

"Wow, this is nice," was the phrase I kept hearing customers comment as I walked through the event. The show covered the entire floor of the Coliseum from one end to the other, and there was something special about the atmosphere. Of course, the classic Christmas songs were playing, and I felt a little like I was Santa himself as I checked out the vendors and the happiness quotient in the room.

THE PROMOTER

Since it was free admission, there was no ticket counter, but Pepsi told me they gave a little over ten thousand six-ounce cups away. I was so proud of the way this fantastic event had turned out because it had stood on its own, not because we were selling bikinis and beer. It was a real family event, the first I'd ever offered. After the event, I heard The Voice again telling me to stay the path, and this would grow. In the meantime, I decided to keep the same once a month flea market, along with the crawfish festival and Labor Day weekend going at the Rice Pavilion, which did include the usual beer and bikinis.

Booking the Rice Pavilion in Gulfport operated by the Harbor Master in the Small Craft Harbor was always an enjoyable experience. The Harbor Master was retired fire chief, Harold Lacy. He was a pleasant man with a good sense of humor; I remember the first time I went in to rent the Pavilion. He had looked at me as if he wasn't quite sure he'd heard me right and said, "You want to rent out the Pavilion for what?"

I had told him, and he just kind of chuckled. He had an extra-large yearly calendar stuck to his door with thumb tacks. Basically, all you did was write in the date you wanted along with whether or not you needed electricity, you paid him a deposit, and that was it! I had walked over to his calendar and picked up the marker, and starting with the January block, I wrote my name on all the dates I needed for the entire year. We soon developed a good relationship, and he always seemed genuinely glad to see me when I came in to place my order.

I learned through this experience that God often speaks through others. I want to remind you that the idea to move into the Coliseum came from an exhibitor at the Rice Pavilion a year earlier, and my sound man helped spark the idea that leads to my becoming a DJ. Sometimes, your most fabulous ideas will come from people that God will place in your path.

Chapter 15
Protests and A Hurricane

> Instead of judging people, why don't you take
> the same time and pray for them,
> to reach out to them, to let them know you believe in them.
> —Joel Olsteen

The 1984 crawfish festival was on the same weekend as the Elks' Crawfish Festival in Biloxi. So, what was in my bag of tricks? You guessed it! Free beer! I created a coupon and placed it in the local paper. It probably cost me less than twenty cents a cup, and the promotion worked. We took in hundreds of coupons, and chances are they ended up buying one or two extras. I added a treasure hunt contest—fifteen keys to the chest hidden throughout the festival—with clues provided on the top of each hour. After all, we wanted them to stay as long as possible! A treasure chest filled with more than $1,500 worth of prizes, including a microwave oven and television teased the audience.

The Beer Was Flowing, and So Was the Money

Last year, I had a problem serving people quickly. I had to fix this; not only was I losing money, but if people had to wait in line, they were not happy campers, and if they left, they might never return. I called my beer distributor and asked him if I opened a keg of beer and let it flow, how long would it take before it would be empty. He told me about fifteen minutes. So, I figured that most kegs I could sell in one hour were four per tap. What that meant was if you had a thousand people in line, you could only serve so many per hour. So that year, I went from two taps of beer to eight taps throughout the festival. Sales dramatically increased as well as profits. When served quickly, people came back more often, which also increased the number of people feeling tipsy faster. All this increased productivity which also increased the demand for the spicy crawfish. After all, what goes better with spicy crawfish, than an ice-cold beer?

It made me realize that had my first festival been a success instead of the complete flop that it was, I wouldn't have been able to handle the crowd. This learning experience happened at just the right time. If I'd had 10,000 customers that day, the chances are good that I'd have lost those patrons for good as they would have never forgotten the long lines waiting for beer.

Here Come the Pesky Christians!

The festivals began to take shape, and I was building a loyal following of customers. As the festivals started getting bigger and rowdier, I began to get Christians coming to my events, telling me they were praying for me. I had many discussions with them about selling beer and the scantily clad women parading around on stage to thunderous applause. I always had the same response, "I am not holding a gun to their head to drink, and the bikinis? Have you been to the beach lately? And besides, if I stopped those two things, I wouldn't make any money, so get lost!"

What bugged me was that some started telling me I was going to hell. I got into a shouting match with a few of them, inviting them to my office to see my picture of Jesus. I wasn't in church at the time, and their behavior didn't exactly have me wanting to run to church either. Someone might ask why I didn't go to church. Shortly after my wife had abandoned our children and me, I went to a priest for consolation. But instead of compassion, he began to lecture me on how the Catholic Church didn't recognize divorce and informed me that I couldn't take communion any longer. I had told him, "No problem. By the way, you're deaf. I told you she left me for another man! I didn't leave the church; the church left me!"

It's not like I woke up thinking, 'how can I make Christians protest me today?' I was doing what I felt was okay and was hurt by these protests. I thought I was a decent person and just wanted to make a few bucks. I reasoned, 'I don't care if it's beer or something else, there will always be folks who don't agree with what you do.' I might have been a bit more responsive if they hadn't told me I was going to hell. In this world, there is no perfect person doing everything correctly. I believed we shouldn't judge people but rather show love, and most of all, pray for those who need guidance or correction. The day would come that I would change, but it wasn't because of the protestors or religious leaders beating me up with, "You're going to hell, Ron Meyers!"

Chapter 16

I Showed Them!

A diamond is a piece of coal that stuck to the job.
—Thomas A. Edison

October 6, 1984, Marquee Cover Story

When the story came out, my hometown newspaper ran a similar story, "Ron Meyers: Making His Mark in the South." My mom called and said she received many calls from former teachers and counselors. They were so happy for me because they thought I was going to end up in jail. God had a plan, and it wasn't that I should be incarcerated. This attention-seeking, arrogant, tireless promoter that did anything for a buck made the Marquee cover along with a story. I'd finally made it, and I'd done it through hard work. What they didn't know was the busier I became, the more it appeared others sought to destroy me. I had rattled so many people with the crawfish festival in Biloxi that people were hoping I would fail. I had to develop a tough skin because behind the scenes; plots were hatching how to take me out of business. It was my encounter with God at an early age that kept part of me confident that my children and I had divine protection. People often said, "You are the luckiest person I ever met." Looking back, it wasn't luck but getting the real-life education that God needed me to receive for something even grander one day. The struggles, the rejections, and the jealousy of others were the ingredients to build my character and tenacity. My drive was never as much about money; but, showing folks that believed I would never amount to anything that they were wrong. God had a plan!

Still, I was wearing a mask, and behind this mask was a man scared of failing my children and scared of failing God. The bigger I was becoming, the more I was looking for ways to hide behind the scenes. To escape the pressure, I began living a secret life of drugs, drinking, and girls that I would tell no one. Looking back, I can see how the hand of God had protected me. Through all of this, His love and mercy were shaping me into the person God created me to be. But before that day came, I would have to be brought to my knees in brokenness.

In the meantime, I had made amends with my mom and dad. When this article came out, it was the first time in my life; my parents said they were proud of me. For five years, I would fly Mom and my grandmother down to Biloxi to experience the Christmas show, and show them around town. I took them to the best restaurants. My grandmother loved the oyster stew at McElroy's, so that was our first stop. God had blessed me financially, so I was able to buy my grandmother a hearing aid, glasses, and a few other things. My mom got anything I could give her. She was happy with just a sweater or a pair of shoes. Again, growing up without fancy things made her not want anything. It was a great moment for me to have time with Mom, and she loved her grandkids. Years later, my daughter went to Iowa for almost a month to take care of my mom before she passed. I have accomplished a lot in life, met a lot of terrific people, but that time I had each year with Mom and Grandma created memories that keep me going today when I think of how much I miss them.

It was on one of these trips Mom had taken me aside and finally admitted how wrong she had been for the way she had treated me. The shock of her words had sent a wave of emotion through me. I had felt the many years of anger and bitterness dissolve like snow in the sun.

I'd looked at her and blew it off as no big deal, "Mom, it's all good. I wouldn't be successful if I didn't grow up the way I did. It gave me the drive to be somebody."

But it had been a big deal. It had released me. Though released from the physical belt that could have ended my life as a child, the invisible noose I had allowed my mother to put around my neck still tugged at me. That day, it had begun to unravel and loosened its grip. From that point on, I practically called my mom every night until God called her home. Healing had taken place. I lost my anger and bitterness towards her and allowed myself to show her that I loved her very much. But even though this forgiveness, though I was able to enjoy my new relationship with my mom, I still couldn't completely turn off her voice from the past. The wounds and hurts from my childhood never seemed to go away, but I was getting stronger.

The Wall Cracked

I made a trip to Denver, Colorado to visit friends and check out the shows there in hopes of getting some fresh ideas for the festivals. I had long since stopped going to mass after a Catholic priest told me that since I'd gotten a divorce, I could no longer participate in communion. But while I was there, my friends convinced me to go with them to an Assembly of God Church. I'd never seen anything like it! There existed such openness and freeness to worship that gave me a completely different perspective as to how some others see God from the Catholic beliefs I knew. Another seed found its way in me that day; this one regarding Protestant viewpoints. In the short time I was there, I felt a little light shine down into the darkness that unbeknownst to me, had been growing there all this time. And the thick concrete wall I'd worked on building so carefully around my heart had started to develop fissures. The struggle within me was far from over. If anything, it had begun to get more intense. There were times I felt so close to God, and that I was so close to finding—something. Then other times, I thought I was on my own again, back in the familiar and temptation would pull me the other way.

Chapter 17

Facing fear in the Face

> Courage is resistance to fear, mastery of Fear, not absence of fear.
> —Mark Twain

Because of the Marquee story, I was now being called a celebrity. It was most certainly directing a lot of my movements. For example, I was enjoying time with the ladies, lots of ladies. I was certainly getting a lot of attention, and for me, that meant life was good, very good. I'd even become a regular at the dance clubs. I was indeed becoming the man about town and saw myself as appearing quite worldly and debonair!

On one such night, my buddy and I were doing the club scene and had a contest, which one of us could dance with the most ladies in one night. At one of our favorite places, the Shy-Anne Social Club in Gulfport, I had just finished dancing with a scorching babe and was ahead by at least five or six girls. After a few beers, I had to take a break, so I left my buddy on the dance floor dancing with his latest babe and was making my way to the restroom when Randy, a very big biker stopped me. No kidding! This dude was tremendous! He towered over me by almost a foot and had to weigh in at least 300 pounds. This guy looked like he could even give the bouncer a run for his money! He was dressed stereotypically in faded blue denim shirt the sleeves looked like they had been ripped off of, a black sleeveless leather jacket full of emblems, a pair of old dirty blue jeans and what I took for work boots. His thin, light brown hair was tousled in several different directions as it looked like it hadn't seen

THE PROMOTER

a comb ever. He got within three inches of me, close enough I could smell the beer on his breath and see the Skoal stuck between his teeth and said, "Mr. Ron Meyers Productions, you think you're so cool, don't you? You out there acting all foolish and silly. You know, I could take you outside and break you like a matchstick."

This moment was a destiny defining moment for me. Was I back in junior high school? Did Gary Peterson move to the south, grow a beard, and gain a few hundred pounds to seek revenge? Was this guy an undercover member of the Elks? I knew I couldn't think about trying to surprise him with a punch. Not only would he probably not even have noticed my feeble attempt at defending myself, but I surely would have been killed. A crowd had gathered around to see what I was going to do. Not having a lot of choices, I knew I had to face fear in the face and said a silent prayer, "Lord, help me."

I looked up, right into the biker's eyes and told him, "Yes, without a doubt, you could. You are much bigger than I am. But what would that prove, that you are some big tough guy who can push people around? My buddy and I are here just having some fun. I don't want any trouble. By the way, God loves you."

I thought to myself, *where did those last three words come from? God loves you? This guy in a bar is about to kill you, and all you can come up with is 'God loves you?'*

To my complete shock, he looked at me with his steel-blue eyes, nodding his head, and said, "Man, I'm going to buy you a beer!"

Still surprised, I couldn't help but give in to my curiosity, "Why would you do that? A minute ago, you wanted to beat me to a pulp."

He replied, "Yea, well, no one has ever stood up to me, and I have pushed people around all my life. Man, I have respect for you."

We sat down and had a brief conversation. It turned out that Randy was a gentle, loving giant! Again, God's favor saved me.

The rest of the story is that six months later, I received a call from his wife, who told me that Randy was terminal with a brain tumor. He had lost a considerable amount of weight and had less than six months to live. She asked if Ron Meyers Productions could help with a fundraiser for his medical bills. A few months later, Randy died. His wife told me that before he died, Randy had accepted Christ. I have thanked God a hundred times for using me in this situation. God knew this man would die soon and had used me to plant the seed of God's love in his heart.

No matter how much I trusted God, I never wanted to be in that situation again. I must also admit some motivation for standing up to Randy. When I was looking at him, my mind transported back to the television show, *Andy Griffith*. Andy had a talk with Opie about a bully who was taking Opie's milk money every day before school. Andy told Opie that sometimes it's better to take a punch rather than run away from a blow. Opie took the punch and proceeded to give the boy what he deserved. The boy never stole his milk money from him again. I thank God I didn't take a punch because I am sure you wouldn't be reading this. Regardless of the circumstances, there comes a time you must face fear and let the chips fall where they may. I have a few friends who ran from fear, and to this day, it stunted their growth in life. Fear will be the biggest enemy on your journey.

Hurricane Elena

After the crawfish festival, I began preparing for my Labor Day Weekend Event, but something just didn't feel right about moving ahead. I had this overwhelming urge to cancel it. And reached for the phone to call my partner.

"Hey, Dusty! It's Ron! I hope I didn't catch you at a bad time," I said when he answered, still tracing my pencil over the Labor Day date on the calendar on my desk.

"What's up?" Dusty replied.

"I got an awful feeling about this show. I can't put my finger on it, but I think we should sit this one out," I said.

"Uh, are you sure about this? That's a lot of money we'll be missing out on," Dusty replied.

"Yea, I know, we might. But something tells me we shouldn't, so I want to go with my gut on this one, but I wanted to get your take on it."

"Hey, you're the boss! If you got a bad feeling, then we're staying home," he agreed.

THE PROMOTER

"Thanks, Dusty," I said, feeling relief as I hung up the phone.

That weekend, August 28, 1985, Hurricane Elena plowed into the coast with winds up to 127 miles per hour, doing 1.3 million dollars' worth of damage to the Gulf Coast. That day my children and I huddled in the middle of our home as the hurricane devoured the roof. Yet I felt a calmness as I looked up into the eye of the storm. But with the tears of the storm also came blessings. It was the end of our stay in low incoming housing as we graduated to an elegant townhouse apartment in Gulfport within walking distance of my office. My two children transferred into one of the best school districts on the coast. Once again, God was looking over me.

> In the eye of the storm, You remain in control
> And in the middle of the war, You guard my soul
> You alone are the anchor, when my sails are torn
> Your love surrounds me in the eye of the storm'
> —from "The Eye of the Storm"
> By Ray Stevenson

Chapter 18
I Get Married Again

---

*"The secret to a happy marriage, is finding
the right person to marry."*
—Ron Meyers

The party life had a toll on me. It was like chasing dust in the wind primarily because I was afraid to have a relationship. I had stayed single nine years after screwing up my first marriage to Denise because I wasn't the most comfortable person with which to share the same roof. I was overbearing and worshiped the almighty dollar. You have heard me share stories about The Voice, but I was committed to The Voice only when I had a problem. When things were right, I only committed to my voice. I was lonely, and the day I turned thirty, I knew I wanted to get married, and I prayed to meet someone that would and could tolerate me in my moments of stupidity, greed, and goofiness. There had been a few girls, but none I wanted to settle down with, and I wanted to settle down. But my problem with dating was, being so well known locally, the same girls that wouldn't give me the time of day a few years prior, acted like best buds when I ran into them.

Finally, I did what I always do when I'm facing a brick wall—I prayed. "Lord, I need to meet someone that isn't from here and has never heard of me." Soon after that prayer, I was eating alone in a pizzeria, and over by the salad bar; I noticed an extremely classy, incredibly good-looking brunette. She was a knockout! I knew I was playing in an entirely different league with this girl. She was going to take my best game yet. So, thinking I too may just need a little salad, I put on my fast-talking promoter face, walked over to the salad bar where she was helping herself, grabbed a bowl, and proceeded to introduce myself.

"Have you ever heard of Ron Meyers Productions?" I asked, using my best ice breaker.

She said, "No, I'm from San Diego."

I thought to myself, *Bingo!* "Let me introduce myself. But first, let me tell you that you are one exquisite young lady! I'm Ron Meyers of Ron Meyers Productions, and I think you would be right for a TV commercial I'm producing for Christmas City. If you think you might be interested, then perhaps we could meet to discuss it?" I inquired, playing it cool. I handed her my card. *Smooth, Ron. You handled that like a pro;* I congratulated myself.

"Thank you, Mr. Meyers," she smiled sweetly and introduced herself.

Wow, did she have a beautiful smile! I thought as I admired her lovely face.

"I may be interested. Let me check my schedule and get back with you," Karen replied. Eyes twinkling, she took my card.

She did call me for that interview, and less than a year later, we were married on October 17, 1987, at Trinity United Methodist Church in Gulfport. I am happy to report that we still are together to this day, proving there is someone out there for everyone. Thank you, Jesus. By the way, I never did put her in a commercial. It was a line just to get her number. I would have, but she's a bit shy.

Dancing Déjà vu

Do you believe God has a sense of humor? I do. A year before I met my wife, Karen, I was on a date with another lady I'd taken to the annual fishing rodeo in Gulfport. Naturally, I had to check out the talent, so we ventured over to the stage where several women were tap-dancing on stage. Having no interest in tap dancers, I stopped just long enough to admire the pretty girls without upsetting my date. Just in case I'd been admiring them just a little too long, I said to her just loud enough to be heard over the music (so I thought), "I wonder when they are going to get some real entertainment around this place!" It was a statement, not a question. Undoubtedly, I had said it not as quietly as I thought as I had upset some very irate mom who came out of the stands to defend her daughter, and she let me have it with both barrels. I told her the dancing showed talent; I just wanted to hear some Rock-n-roll, some *Freebird* or something. A year later, when I met Karen's mom, it turned out to be that same mom I'd offended that day! Karen was a dance instructor and was one of the dancers I stopped to admire. Everything was good, and she was a great mother-in-law. She left this world too early, but I had the pleasure of her helping with my events.

Chapter 19

The Swimsuit Calendar and More Protests

> I am not in competition with anybody but myself.
> My goal is to beat my last performance.
> —Celine Dion

My sixth crawfish festival was going to compete with the Biloxi Crawfish Festival once again. My dates for the festival were selected back in January, this time, it was not intentional to be on the same weekend, but I must admit I enjoyed it. Determined to outdo them, I decided that the sixth crawfish festival was going to be the best one yet. The cash prize for the Bikini contest increased to $1,000 in cash, plus lots of prizes. I also planned to produce a Gulf Coast first-ever "Sports Illustrated-like" calendar featuring winners from the bikini contest. Some of the most beautiful girls on the coast had registered to participate. Of course, there was some talk by the rumor mill that I would never do a calendar that it was just a publicity stunt; started, I believe, by my friendly competition.

I brought in the best local and regional entertainment like Jerry Fisher and the Music Co. with Debbie Stanbro, Bobby Cure and the Summertime Blues, Doug Mays and the Key West Coconuts, and the Louisiana Group Atchafalaya. And to enhance the live entertainment, I stationed two big-screen TVs in the Rice Pavilion to capture stage action, since I knew it would be an overflow crowd on the outdoor staging area. Oh yes! This was going to be great!

Even though I thrived on competition, my focus was being the best at what I was doing. Competition is a way of life, and I knew to achieve my goals, I couldn't allow myself to dwell on what a big, powerful fraternal organization was doing. Instead, I focused on providing fun, family, community, and an event that people would say something positive about when they left. And most of all, an event that would be good for the City of Gulfport. I did notice that a few of the Elks members were sneaking around to see how big our crowd was. Nothing unusual. I believe I mentioned I often sent my guys to check them out as well. However, I couldn't help but stir the pot a little for them once on stage, "Doesn't Gulfport have the best crawfish festival in the state of Mississippi?"

The crowd, all fired up from the beer, screamed, "Yes!"

Yup, that was satisfying, I thought, smiling to myself as I saw them look up at me as I was standing on the stage and scowl.

Those pesky Christians were back. I think I really must have pulled their tail this time with the swimsuit calendar and the skimpy suits. One of them called out, "Hey, Hugh Hefner! Do your naked girls come with benefits?" Another hollered, "You're going to Hell Ron Meyers!"

I said, "Really? Get some glasses! My girls aren't naked!" After I said that, I got this weird feeling. Those words seemed louder to me than they should have been, almost echoing in my head, and I got a strange sensation in the pit of my stomach. I can't quite explain. I thought to myself, *I just referred to them as my girls. Maybe I am going to Hell.* I brushed it aside and asked one of the pesky Christians, "If it is so offensive, why are you coming and watching the most 'offensive' part?"

The one that seemed to be the leader of the small group piped up, "I had to see it with my own eyes. Besides, it's the best time to give these lost souls Bible tracts! Letting those young girls parade around up there with barely anything on is offensive! Wise up, Meyers! The money isn't worth it!"

There it was, that feeling again. I brushed it aside. "If it bothers you so much, put on a blindfold so you won't be offended! Leave me alone, or I'll give you your admission back and have you escorted out!" I bluffed, yelling back at him. There wasn't anything I could do; they did pay their admission fee.

I knew I was probably in the wrong for thinking so, but when I glanced in his direction from the stage, I couldn't help but chuckle as it sure looked like he was having fun to me! He sure wasn't preaching! I thought to myself, *maybe he's worried about the rapture, but, of course, I wouldn't want to judge.* I laughed a little at my cleverness, but it was a nervous, uneasy laugh.

The Girls of the Gulf Coast Calendar is Finished, and It is a Beauty!

Symba Smith, Our Cover Girl

The full-color calendar was finally finished, and boy was it a beauty! We held the calendar premiere on Saturday, August 28, at Gayfers in Edgewater Mall with the girls who had posed for it on hand to autograph copies. I did a total of sixteen months because I wanted to get it into the stores as soon as possible. The women featured on the pages of the calendar were: Renee Barhanovich, Julie Ann Bath, Heidi Brockmeyer, and Gia Sekul—all of Biloxi; Charissa Penton of Ocean Springs; Marianna Whittingham, Rachel Carter, Laura Olier, Angie Snowden, and Symba Smith—all of Gulfport; Andrea Williams of Picayune; Teresa Grubbs of Poplarville; Paula Dent of Waveland; and, Barbie Russum of Long Beach.

Since some of the girls were from prominent families, there weren't any protests when the calendar came out. It was a beautiful calendar, and each shot reflected the girls tastefully. It promoted the

Gulf Coast as a premier destination with lovely girls on our beautiful beaches. I touted it as a help for tourism, and it served as a springboard to launch some of the girls into new careers. For instance, our cover girl, Symba Smith from Gulfport, she went on to win the spokesmodel category on *Star Search* with Ed McMahon. If you Google her name today, you will see her name connected with many films in Hollywood.

Some of the swimsuit calendars were distributed as gifts to friends, with some ending up in the hands of various radio personalities. I did some phone interviews around the country about the calendar, which prompted an explosion of interest in people wanting to know about the Gulf Coast, crawfish, and our beaches. It was a calendar that was flying off the shelf.

As I sat at my desk between calls just after the calendar had come out, I'd flipped through it, remembering that during its production, I had added motivational quotes each month. I had never told anyone, but one of my future ambitions was to perhaps one day become a motivational speaker. My finger had traced one of the motivational quotes I'd written above the lovely girl smiling back at me, and I'd felt it again; that war; that war going on in me with the devil on one shoulder, the angel on the other. It didn't escape me that it was happening more often and seemed louder, closer as if someone was turning the volume up. Even as much as I craved it, the added success and notoriety from the turmoil boiled inside of me. It was getting harder and harder to thump that angel off my shoulder when it began to nag me. Though I would fight it, it would just fly right back up there, nudging me until I invariably found myself coming back to the same question, "Are those Christians, right? Am I going to Hell?" Whether I liked it or not, the Christians had stirred up something in me. I felt the mask I'd been wearing begin to crack. I caught my reflection in the glass of the picture I'd had on my desk of J.R. Ewing and almost asked myself out loud, almost involuntarily, "Who am I?"

Chapter 20

Here They Come, After the Christmas Show!

Stay True to yourself. An original is worth more than a copy.
—Suzy Kassem

As you'll remember, when I started Ron Meyers Productions, I tried to tap into the Elks Crawfish Festival. It didn't work, but it still worked out. However, I'd just gotten wind that there was a promoter trying to tap into my Christmas event! I had stopped at a Krispy Kreme to pick up some donuts and coffee and was looking at the trades while sitting in line in my car, and there it was, plastered in the events section. On October 29–30, 1988, Southern Productions of Mississippi was to host "The First Christmas Craft Fair of the 1988 Season" two weeks before my Christmas show, and I was furious! I paid for my purchase, and throwing the coffee into the seat, and cramming the donuts into the cup holder; I took off for my office. The coffee lid had come open, and coffee dripped from the passenger seat and down onto the floor mat and had left little rivers cascading down the passenger door. The once jelly donuts soaked the bag thoughtlessly crammed into the cup holder. Having quite suddenly lost my appetite after reading the article, I never even noticed.

I went straight to my office and called the number for Bill Holmes, the director of the Coliseum, who was also the organizer for the Elks' Crawfish Festival.

A female voice answered, "Mississippi Coast Coliseum, this is Michelle, how may I help you?"

"I'd like to speak with Bill Holmes please," I was doing my best to keep a cool head and not take it out on his receptionist.

"May I ask who's calling, please?"

"It's Ron Meyers."

"Hold, please."

A moment later, Bill was on the phone, "Bill Holmes speaking."

"Bill, this is Ron Meyers. What's the deal? Are you trying to get even with me for that Crawfish festival a million years ago? Are you putting on a Christmas show two weeks before my event?"

"Ron, I can't control who rented the building," he responded calmly. "Besides, didn't you just have your crawfish festival the same day we had ours here?"

I didn't buy his answer for a second. Now convinced he was seeking revenge, I quipped, "My date was picked months before that one. It was written on the event calendar if you'd bothered to look. It was not intentional."

"Well, I don't make the decisions on who does what and when. I'm sorry you have a problem with it, but what can I say? My hands are tied."

Angry, I hung up the phone, resisting the temptation to break it. I glared at my picture of J.R., then smiled. What he didn't know was that my Christmas Arts and Crafts Fair was going through a transformation. Let Southern Productions have their festival. I would deal with this competition in my own way.

I was inspired while attending a church program with my family in December 1987. Decorated with cottages cut from wood, delightfully painted and decorated, complete with artificial snow, lights, and decorated trees, the alter was beautiful that year! When I saw it, I told my wife that I was going to add that to my Christmas show. I wanted to do something different, something no one else had ever done. The vision was so clear! I knew without a doubt after finding out what the competition was up to; this was a divine idea. I was going to transform the Christmas City Craft Sale into Christmas City USA, into something unbelievably beautiful! I'd turn it into a magical shopping experience no one would ever forget! I truly believed God knew that Southern Productions planned to infringe on my successful event and inspired me with the idea that was not only phenomenal but would put Christmas City USA on the cover of the Marquee. God, my faithful friend, was once again looking out for my family and me.

Christmas City USA Debuts on November 11–12, 1988

Ron & Karen Meyers

I hired Gulf Coast artist, Gary Stover, a thirty-seven-year-old designer who was the art director for Collegiate Marketing in Gulfport and shared my vision for Christmas City with him. He knew just what to do, and the more we brainstormed, the more Christmas City grew. I was renting a warehouse in Gulfport, and he started in August and worked up until the event. We bought hundreds of cans of spray paint, glitter, pillow stuffing, and fifty twelve-foot foam core boards. We added the North Pole with a children's game and movie room, a cafeteria, continuous music, and an information booth disguised as City Hall, holiday style. I was the Mayor of Christmas City, and it was a city with no politics, only a city that created a positive shopping experience. It didn't take much for the exhibitors to catch the spirit, and they happily joined in adding their touches in holiday decorating.

Before Christmas City USA's debut, Gary had told me when we had finished putting up the sets, "It's a dream come true…bigger than life! I have always loved fantasy. I would much rather do this kind of thing that makes people smile than toil at a desk all day."

Looking at what he'd done with wood, paint, glitter, and Styrofoam, there was no denying that Gary was an incredible artist. He turned the arena into a life-size holiday village complete with street signs, snow-covered cottages, old-fashioned street lamps, real pine trees, and Santa himself. I was in awe of all that Gary created from such ordinary materials and pure imagination. Looking at this magical city as it sparkled beneath the coliseum lights, I felt like I imagined Walt Disney himself must have felt after he had envisioned Disneyland and then watched it come to life for the very first time. I gasped in awe as I told Gary, "Christmas is people's favorite time of year; just wait until they see the entrance and this city!" We both knew it was going to be positive for the future of the show's growth.

Gary Stover is no longer with us now, but I am so grateful for God putting us in each other's path. Gary used his gifts and talents that helped create an event that is still going on today. For several years after that initial opening, Gary's work brought many smiles to children and shoppers alike. Sadly, time eventually took its toll on the sets, and they were retired to a higher purpose as you'll find out about a little later in the book.

Christmas City Hits the Road!

That year, I received a call from the manager of the Louisiana Superdome who invited us to bring Christmas City to New Orleans. In the first year, we held the show in the upstairs meeting rooms, but in the second year, we were allowed to rent half the floor. It would be a monumental task setting up the hundreds of booths, but we were up for it! I looked out across the field, completely awestruck. This same floor would be covered with artificial grass and played on by the New Orleans Saints! Let me tell you, standing on that floor of the New Orleans Superdome was an incredible moment! Looking up into the stands, I couldn't help but think this was not too shabby for a juvenile delinquent from Iowa with no college degree, only a passion and desire to make his mark the world. I was here! The fact that I was producing an event in one of the largest markets in the United States was most definitely a thank you God moment!

The show also traveled to The Mobile Civic Center in Mobile, Alabama that year and for three years after, as well as the Forrest County Multi-purpose center in Hattiesburg, Mississippi, for one year.

Chapter 21
Lord, My Son Needs a Miracle

> That your faith should not stand in the wisdom
> of men but in the power of God.
> —1 Corinthians 2:5 (KJV)

Karen and I celebrated the birth of Ryan Lewis Meyers on September 15, 1989. Four months later, we were at Texas Children's Hospital. His diagnosis, with a rapid heartbeat, turned our world upside down. The doctors approached us with an experimental drug for his rare condition. The FDA hadn't approved it, but the doctors were optimistic. After signing a boatload of forms, they administered the new drug to our son.

I was holding my precious tiny son and imagining the worst. I kept telling him, "Daddy is here, and I will never leave you." I had so many crazy thoughts going through my head. *Is it my fault? God, are you punishing me for something I did? Can I donate money to a church?* I went through the usual things you do with God when you find yourself in such a circumstance—over-analyzing everything I'd ever done wrong in my life, begging, pleading, bargaining. Of course, most of what I was going through in my head wasn't doing anything but driving me nuts, and I knew you couldn't buy God's help. But I wasn't thinking straight. I knew He wasn't punishing me, but there was a lesson in all of this. Though I would have gladly given my own life for my son, this was one of those things that I realized I had no control over. I was guilty of relinquishing power to God when things got tough, but when the ship started to sail on an even keel, I'd grab the wheel again as if to say, "Thank you, God, I'll take it from here." It was a huge realization to accept that this was one situation that there would be no taking the wheel back from Him by me.

I'm one of those people who has been guilty many times of micromanaging situations. "Wait, what are you doing? You're not doing it right. Let me do it," is, I hate to say it, but kind of, somehow… well, it became one of my mantras. It wasn't anything for me to lose my temper if you weren't doing whatever I asked of you to my satisfaction, nor did it matter that I may be being unreasonable. It may not matter that I didn't give you all the information and may have even had no idea what you had accomplished on the task before I jumped on you. In my eyes, for whatever reason it hit me, I could blow just because I thought you weren't fast enough. But this time, I could do absolutely nothing but hand the situation and my son over to God in complete patience, pray He would fix it, and prepare myself to accept His will whatever the outcome. I had no choice but to let Him do it His way, in His time, with absolutely no help or direction from me. It was one of the hardest things I've ever had to do in my life. When I see something that needs fixing, I want to fix it. I couldn't fix this. I was able to finally calm down when I stopped and reminded myself of all the times that Jesus had helped me, and everything had worked out.

We were staying in the hospital room with Ryan in Houston, and every morning, I would get up early and walk into the downtown area for coffee and prayer. This morning I prayed, "Lord, for my sanity, tell me something, anything." I went outside the coffee shop and sat on a bench watching the traffic with tears in my eyes when it came—A peace that engulfed my whole body. And I knew without a doubt; it was going to be okay. Then the whisper of God reminded me of how much He loved His Son, and then something was whispered that comforted me beyond any explanation, "Ron, I love you and I will never leave you or your family."

As I meditated on those words, I understood several different messages as relayed to me. God showed me that how I held my tiny son as if I could will him to live was how He had held me in that closet when I was 11 years old when I'd tried to commit suicide. That was a powerful revelation to me. I got up from the bench and walked back to the hospital and told my wife it was going to be okay; God was with our Son. She then told me how her wonderful grandparents had started a prayer chain at their church in San Diego and that soon thousands of people from all over the world would be praying for little Ryan. After a few weeks, we brought Ryan home to Gulfport wearing a heart monitor, which he would wear for a few years.

Today, I'm happy to say that Ryan is doing well and is a thriving young entrepreneur in his own right. While writing this book, he married a beautiful woman of God, Jamie Hebert, on June 23, 2019. Thank you, Jesus!

Chapter 22
My Conscience Was Pricked

"For we are His workmanship, created in Christ
Jesus for good works, which God prepared
beforehand that we should walk in them."
—Ephesians 2:10 (NKJV)

"Oh, my Sweet Aunt Martha! Have you seen that crowd out there!" Albert exclaimed as he came into the office to grab a few more boxes of cups to load into the concession trailer. Gwen laughed at his remark as she headed into the backroom to count the latest draw, and I grinned as I headed for the stage to introduce the best entertainment act I'd booked so far, none other than the nationally famous "Toto." Over twenty thousand would attend over the next three days. It was unbelievable! The bikini girls were as beautiful and enticing as ever in their dental floss swimsuits. The beer was flowing like waterfalls; so much so, the police arrested people all night long.

"How about that, folks! Wouldn't you like to take this one home to mama!" I baited the audience as a gorgeous curvaceous hottie stepped onto the stage in five-inch silver high heels flashing a white smile that virtually glowed from her dark tan. Her platinum blonde hair swung about her shoulders as she made a few turns on the stage, showing off her incredible physique in a silver swimsuit that left very little to the imagination. She teased the crowd, which went hog wild.

"Let's hear it for Melanie Craft! Remember, your applause is your vote, so make it loud if you think Melanie should go home with the prize!" I shouted into the microphone, but the crowd was already so loud, my last few words faded into their revelry.

"She's alright, but my girl is better!" shouted some guy in a mullet, tan shorts and dockers in front of me right below where I stood on stage, slinging his red cup of beer for emphasis.

"Well, I like this one!" a guy in a backward black baseball cap and a glowing green muscle shirt with a Nike symbol on it dressed in blue jean knee-high cuts offs and flip flops yelled back.

"Oh yeah? Well, I KNOW my girl is better! And she's gonna win! Judy! Judy! Judy!" he yelled, trying to entice the crowd to join in. On the back of the stage where the other girls who had already competed waited for everyone to have their turn on the runway, a gorgeous redhead in a yellow polka dot string bikini waved enthusiastically at the crowd.

The second guy threw a punch, and the next thing I knew, they were crashing against the stage, and several more had joined. It scared the daylights out of me as I saw the first guy come back with a cut below his eye and blood streaming down his face but refusing to back down to the second guy. The mixture of blood, beer, and flying fists had become terrifying as the girls on stage screamed.

Dusty tried to stop one of the festival-goers who had joined in the fight. I saw him duck just in time to keep from getting hit as the intended punch slammed into the guy standing behind him, sending him sprawling into the metal chairs and ending up in a heap on the ground.

I tried to yell to Dusty, but the noise had become deafening, made worse by the addition of police whistles and sirens. I looked over at the concession stand to see Wilber and Albert crouching behind their bar, their heads popping up just enough to keep tabs on what was going on. It was in this middle of this chaos I started to hear the words of the Christian protesters echoing in my mind, "You are causing people to get drunk and fight. You should be ashamed of yourself!" I wondered then if my conscious was beginning to wake up as instead of judging them as just being incredibly annoying, I'd started to think that maybe they had been right.

THE PROMOTER

It wasn't long before the Gulfport Police Auxiliary showed up and arrested all the troublemakers, and the festival went on as though nothing had happened. I still felt uneasy even after the event when we met back in the hotel room.

"Hey, pass that thing over here, will you!" Stephen said. He was a young guy who had joined us for this event as one of our regulars was sick.

Wilber passed him the joint, as Albert popped another beer. "Man! What did you think about that fight, huh?" Albert asked incredulously. "That was the third one today, and the closest one we had you where you might just have to share the stage!" he laughed.

Gwen had finished the tally of all the beer-soaked money laid out across the bed. She would carry it in a small suitcase she would carry with her through the parking lot to her car as always after the event so she could deposit it the next day. Jimmy, being Jimmy, took a flying leap into the middle of it and threw a handful in the air. "Have you ever seen so much money in your life?" Unfortunately, seeing all that green floating in the air and back down onto the bed again was all it took for me to decide I could live with those Christian protesters. Gwen took a magazine and swatted at Jimmy and started raking it all into the suitcase.

The Warning

A few months later, it was business as usual. I forgot the protesters, and we put on our annual shrimp festival. It was a sweltering June day with most people not wearing shirts, and I was walking among the crowd, laughing and shaking hands as always and making sure everyone was having a great time in between sets of entertainment. As the day wore on and the sun began to set across the Gulf that Friday night, the crowd started to change to a little rowdier bunch. What happened next will be something forever etched in my mind. As I had mentioned, a war had been going on inside of me for quite some time now, so I had gone from calloused to somewhat sensitive when something came at me full force. Enough of my armor had cracked, that these attacks were now convicting me that what I was doing wasn't right.

I turned around to find myself standing in front of a patron with no shirt and a tattoo that covered his entire back. For a few seconds, time seemed to slow, the music seemed to stop, and I felt sick at my stomach as I stared at this man's back in front of me. Nothing else seemed to exist, not the crowds, not the band, or the girls in bikinis, nothing but me and this guy's back and the voice of the Christians. The guy looked over his shoulder straight at me, grinning, then laughed at me. I can't possibly describe the chill this had given me. The tattoo had been an elaborately drawn picture of a devil having sex with an angel. My blood had run icy cold, and I physically shivered. I had no doubt what-so-ever, this was my wake-up call. Terrified, right there on the spot, I silently prayed, "God, I don't like this anymore. I want out!"

That guy's ink had a traumatic effect on me. I knew it was no coincidence that I had seen that. I was scared, and I started increasing my use of pot more, trying to block out the battle inside of me. I was going through the motions at work and at home. I knew I was ready for a change, but how? How would I replace the revenue that was keeping my offices open and supporting my family? I felt like I had no one to talk to about this war inside of me. So many people depended on me, but I wasn't kidding myself. I knew the hell hounds were after me, but where I had felt like I had everything under control, now I felt like they had gotten just a little too close for comfort, and I was getting that 'cornered' feeling. I began to pray like never before, "Lord, I don't know what to do. This isn't fun anymore. I don't know how to get out. You must do something!"

I knew I would not have another festival until next year. I canceled the shrimp festival for the following year and relied on our crawfish festival and Christmas City USA. I started going to church more often, and I was praying for Godly intervention. I never told a soul, not even my wife, what I was going through. When you battle with your conscience, it is like the old cartoon I was talking about earlier, where you have a devil on one shoulder and an angel on the other, continually telling you what to do. It's something very personal that, for the most part, you find yourself doing completely alone. I knew something had to happen, but I didn't know what. The only thing that kept me calm was pot. I wasn't a drinker, but pot relaxed me and numbed the torture within.

Let's face it when life is good; nobody thinks about changing. Only when things go wrong, terribly wrong, we start looking for a way out. One of the most common questions I am often asked these days is, "If there is a God, why are so many bad things happening in my life?" The answer is simple; not many people turn to God when life is all peachy. It's in the trials that we begin to seek God. Does that mean He causes them? No, He allows them and is reaching out to us with help. My problem was, I was so dependent on the money that I wasn't ready to trade cash for God. That year, my mask cracked, and I was positively leaking with insecurities. The question was, what was it going to take for me to surrender and remove my mask? The good news is, God never gives upon us! Not even a stubborn old sinner like me.

Chapter 23

My Mom Died

> We are confident, yes, well pleased rather to be absent
> from the body and to be present with the Lord.
> —2 Corinthians 5:8 (NKJV)

In September of 1995, I got a phone call from my mom who told me she had stage four colon cancer. Thirty days later, October 17, 1995, I got a call from the hospital that at only fifty-nine years old, my mom had died. She had left this earth way too young. This date also happened to be the same day as my wedding anniversary. Driving to the office, I struggled with this and prayed for God's guidance, "God, why of all days, why did Mom have to die on my anniversary?"

There was no delay this time in His response as I heard The Voice tell me, "Ron, a change is coming."

That's it. No big sermon, lecture, or anything came that gave me any change in direction. I flew home a few times before mom passing to see what I could do to help. I remember one day while driving her to the doctor; she was telling me how much pain she was suffering. I asked her, "Mom, do you want me to go find you some marijuana?"

She looked at me and started laughing, and I will never forget her answer, "Why would I want that?"

I told her it was better than the morphine they were giving her. She laughed during the rest of the trip to the doctor's office. As we walked into the doctor's office, she was still thinking about it as she said, "Leave it to you to say something like that!"

THE PROMOTER

In the last few weeks of her life, my daughter, Dawn, went to Iowa to be with my mom. They had put my mom on hospice in her home, and my daughter did everything for her. Mom called Dawn, her guardian angel.

The day of Mom's passing, Dawn had told me she had been lying in her bed dressed in a pale pink cotton gown. Her face had become taunt and drawn, and her color was sallow between the pain and destruction ravaging her body. My daughter, Dawn, was there holding her hand as my mom's time grew short. She had told me that suddenly, Mom's eyes had become huge as she looked up into the corner of the ceiling of her bedroom closest to the bed and said very plainly, "Mom!" A few moments later, she died.

Was she hallucinating? Or was her mom comforting her before she joined her, waiting to escort her to Heaven? I have no idea, but years later, when I was on the radio, I interviewed many people who had also had a near-death experience and all of them without exception had said that a loved one had come to get them. I know the Bible doesn't address this. All I know is my mom, who had cancer all over her body and was in tremendous pain, died with a big smile on her face.

Because I didn't appear to show much emotion during Mom's funeral, during the wake, a few people had come up to me and made a comment, "You must not have been close to your mom."

I asked why in the world would they say that. These curious people had replied because I was cheerful instead of a complete basket case, and no one had seen me cry. I explained that I very much loved my mom. I knew how she had suffered, and I was content that she is finally at peace. We had a great relationship over the past few years. I treated my mom the best I could. I had helped her financially, and I called her every night. I did everything a good son would do. I had no regrets. Most importantly, I know where she is and that she isn't in pain or suffering anymore, and I have no doubt I will be reunited with her one day.

Chapter 24
My Party's Over!

> Be careful what you pray for, you just might get it!
> —Unknown

The following year, it was time for the crawfish festival, and again, the beer, pot, bikinis, and fights continued. Even after all that had happened, I couldn't find it in me to stop the last show at which I continued to sell beer. I needed the money. I had prayed for God to do something, and from what I could tell, He wasn't doing anything. Or was He? Was God working behind the scenes to change my destiny one more time? God created my personality, and He knew that I couldn't be convinced to do something I didn't want to do, especially when I had made up my mind to be stubborn and do the exact opposite. But this time, my motivation wasn't out of pride or defiance, but out of fear—fear of losing a sure income.

During this personal turmoil, the City of Gulfport had been meeting behind closed doors about changing the rent structure for events at the Rice Pavilion. Since I produced most of the coast events, this was explicitly aimed at me. A few city officials wanted to pass a new rental plan, and rumors were circulating that Mr. Coliseum Director was going after my crawfish festival and was trying to influence the powers that be in Gulfport. The new rental plan required a percentage of all admission fees, a percentage of beer sales, and a percentage of crawfish sales instead of charging me a flat rental fee. I went to the City Council meeting that day with my attorney to fight this. The room was packed with people who weren't necessarily interested in things that had to do with my case, but other things that were going on as well. The council members, dressed in casual business attire, sat in a semicircle behind a large light wooden wall, the American and Mississippi State flags behind them. Despite the air conditioning, the room was warm as we waited for our turn. We didn't have to wait long. The Speaker brought up the motion proposing the rent change as calmly as if he were only suggesting a change in the brand of toilet paper they should buy next month.

I suddenly stood up and exploded, "Why would you do this? Because I am making money, you want more? Where were you in the early days when I was losing money?"

The dull din of voices was suddenly replaced with the sound of squeaking chairs as people turned to see what the ruckus was about. I exclaimed angrily between gritted teeth, "If you pass this, I will never do another event in the Rice Pavilion!"

As we left City Hall, stepping from the fluorescent-lit rooms into the bright sunshine, my attorney looked at me and said, "They are going to pass it."

"Really? Why do you think that?" I asked him, blinking in the bright sunlight and running my hand through my hair, still perturbed from the confrontation. Seagulls called obliviously from the air above.

"Because they don't believe you will walk away from that kind of money," he replied as he looked at me seriously.

"Is that so! Well, if that's what they think, then they are underestimating me!" I defended; my face clouded in renewed anger.

I'd been in my office going over some bills when I got the call that afternoon, letting me know they had passed it.

"The party's over!" I yelled at the walls in my office after I hung up the phone with a mixture of trepidation, fear, and oddly—relief. I had received the answer to my prayer. I knew it was going to take something drastic for me to change, and I had told God I wanted out, but I just never would have thought it would end the way that it did.

You would think that when God answers prayer, you will jump around in excitement, but I didn't. I was scared, seriously scared.

Inside I was quivering, absolutely in fear of the future! I had my Christmas City Show, but was that enough money to survive? How would I support my family if it wasn't? I thought about all those nights my crew and I had laughed and joked and counted wads of money sometimes so soaked with beer we had to pull them apart literally. I thought about the great times we'd had together, all the people I'd met and hung out with famous people. And I thought about the bad times too—the fights, the protestors, those who would have done anything to see me brought down and not the least of which, the time I'd missed away from my family when they'd had things like birthday parties and family trips without me because I couldn't leave. I wouldn't miss those. But wrong or not, this was all I knew, and I wondered, *what in the world am I going to do now?*

Remembering I'd always wanted to be a motivational speaker, I joined a company called Success Motivation Institute, and I was holding success workshops and teaching people about goal setting and time management. It wasn't quite the same thing, but it was enjoyable. I was recruiting individuals and training them to become successful coaches, but compared to what I'd done before, the money was minimal. Even so, though I was still smoking pot to drown out the hurt and fear of the unknown, I did notice I wasn't smoking it as often. Yet, I had never let go and let God, and I didn't have the courage to trust Him enough to do so now. I wanted to, but I didn't want it bad enough because I was still trying to 'run my show.' I was also still wrestling with the protestors in my head telling me I was going to Hell. The tug of war in my mind had intensified as much as the one in my heart, and I still thought the only way to ease it was smoking pot. It didn't help matters that the Coliseum did a crawfish festival soon after this, booking some of the entertainment that had played at my festivals each year. Coincidence? I didn't think so either, but only God knows.

October of 1998, my wife and I suffered her second miscarriage, and I was losing hope. I kept things to myself because I didn't want lectures or judgment from people. I had gone back to the office a few days later and found myself going back in my mind to that day when God first spoke to me as I'd sat at the bottom of my closet. I looked up at the picture of Jesus on the wall and said to Him, "Lord, I sure hope you were right about being with me because I feel so alone right now. I do want to do great things for you."

Even though my life up to this point might not have reflected it, in the still quietness of my office, I knew I meant it. I knew for me to change, God had to close one door so that I would walk through another door, His door. By the way, this wouldn't be the first door He closed.

Chapter 25
The Day I Surrendered

> He shall call upon Me, and I will answer him; I will be
> with him in trouble; I will deliver him and honor him.
> —Psalm 91:15 (NKJV)

On this day, I was preparing to go to Columbia, South Carolina, for a Success Convention, and I was looking forward to the drive so I could think. Even the radio had seemed to irritate me, so I'd turned it off and spent most of the trip in silence as the highway lines slipped rhythmically past me. I felt a little better as I couldn't help but admire the beauty of the Appalachian Mountains as I passed through them. I needed a break, so I stopped at a little old-fashioned General Store along the way and wandered in to relieve myself and to look around. There were bins of fruit and individually wrapped candy, and on the counters were baked goods and hoops and stacks of all kinds of cheeses and crackers. Shallow wooden shelves beneath the stands and between the bins held every type of handmade preserves you could imagine. There were also colorful jellies, pickles, and sauces; their lids adorned with fabric gingham and ribbons. An old cooler was nearby full of bottled root beer, ginger beer, and drinks with labels I hadn't seen in many years, Handmade toys and tools, as well as gimmicky tourist trap items and more handmade candy, in bags this time, hung on the walls. I stood staring at the vast selection of candy. There were packages of many flavored licorices, bright-colored hand-pulled taffies, caramels, and lemon drops, among others I'd remembered from my childhood. And for just a second, I was a boy again, standing in my grandparent's yard with all my cousins surrounding me laughing, anticipating the fall of coins glittering in the sun as my grandfather's hands tossed them in the air.

"Good afternoon, Sir. Can I help you find something?" an elderly gentleman with kind eyes woke me from my daydream.

"Oh, no, thank you. I was just looking at the candy, trying to decide which kind my children would like best," I answered. Smiling nostalgically, I pulled a few packages from the wall for my wife and children. I grabbed a bag of brightly colored cellophane-wrapped sourballs for myself, remembering they had been one of my favorites as a boy. After paying for them and thanking the man, I left the store, stepping down off the small wooden porch shaded by huge trees on either side of it and behind. I blinked from the bright sunlight as I stepped into the small gravel parking lot in front of the store and hesitated as I reached for the handle of my car. Taking a deep breath of the fresh mountain air, I took one last look around me, noticing the sounds of many songbirds as I looked around at the mountain landscape. It was so beautiful here!

I enjoyed the rest of the trip to South Carolina with new eyes as I appreciated the deep green valleys, the calm, sparkling lakes reflecting the clouds above, the towering mountains and rolling hills, and white-capped rivers flowing over beds of glittering golden stones. I also admired the quaint small towns I passed by and through; the farmers on their tractors in the fields, roadside fruit stands. I even made a point to enjoy the lonely sound of a train whistle as I watched a train pass in front of me instead of swearing impatiently when my journey was interrupted. I'd been places that were beautiful before; as I mentioned earlier in the book, I'd made many trips to Colorado. But I think I was always in such a hurry; I don't think I ever took the time to notice what was outside of my car windows, having my mind intent on whatever I was to do at my destination and worrying more about paying attention to road signs. Most of the time, if I took the time to look at something, I was analyzing it as to how I could make a buck from it. But this trip had been different. It was if I was really noticing the detail in God's creation for the very first time and now wondered, how could I possibly have not seen? With fresh eyes,

I couldn't help but consider the beauty of God's handiwork and the care He had taken to make something so incredibly wonderous that my words could in no way capture the way I felt as it stirred something new in me.

The convention was pleasant but unremarkable, and on the way home, I picked Atlanta as my overnight stop. After unloading my car and checking into the hotel room, I was hungry. Not finding anything appealing on the hotel menu, I decided to go back to a barbeque place I'd seen not far from the hotel for barbeque and bring it back to the room. As it was a Saturday evening, the streets were packed with cars and the sidewalks with people beneath the bright lights of the city going to and fro. It seemed everyone in Atlanta was out looking for a good time. I didn't even feel a temptation to join them.

Every so often, I'd pass a place with a line of people standing outside of a door, and I could hear the faint sound of music coming from it. I had my window rolled partway down, and the air was full of a mixture of the smell of car exhaust, cigarettes, and good food. I slowed down to avoid a cop car with its lights on and saw two policemen wrestling with a man lying face down on the sidewalk as a small group of people watched. It struck me odd how most people walked right on by them as if this required no more of their attention than as if a piece of paper had blown in front of them. Finding the barbeque place, I pulled in, got my food, and drove back to the hotel room uneventfully. I was a bit restless, but it wasn't anything a little pot wouldn't cure.

The next morning, I turned on the television, and Charles Stanley, the pastor at First Baptist Church in Atlanta, Georgia, was on. I sat down and lit up my joint to relax before the drive home. It was about halfway through his program, I just kind of matter-of-factly said out loud, "You know, God, I have everything I thought I ever wanted. I have recognition, I've been in the newspapers, made some money, but I am miserable. What's the story?"

A New Person

Then it happened. I heard it—the clear, beautiful, and precious voice inside which I hadn't heard in so long now, I had almost wondered if I had ever really heard it at all, "Ron, now that I have your attention, listen to me and I will show you your destiny. It is time to promote Me!"

This time, The Voice produced a warm feeling. I had chill bumps. It is difficult to explain, and it may sound like a cliché, but The Voice did bring life into my dead soul! It brought my hope alive again to the point; I genuinely felt like I did when I was that kid, so many years ago, who was running and laughing with my cousins in the warm summer sunshine as we ran for ice cream and candy after collecting my grandfather's coins. The feeling was that good! It was real, not from the pot, not from the barbeque ribs from the night before. I felt the Spirit of God! It compelled me to flush the joint down the toilet, repent, and rededicate my life to Christ. That day, I went from a knowledge of Jesus to the beginning of a love relationship with Jesus. And this time, I knew my life would truly change.

I felt I was given another chance—a chance to move from a life of selfishness and self-indulgence. I knew I'd been living to a life that had real purpose and meaning. I didn't just feel refreshed like I had remembered feeling when I breathed in that mountain air at the General Store I had stopped at in the Appalachians; I felt I was the one who was fresh! I felt my past erased and that I now had a new canvas on which to paint the life that God had for me. Only this time, I would allow Him to control the paintbrush. So, what would my future hold now? I'm glad I had no idea because if God gave me a glimpse, there is no way I would have believed it. The hand of God was about to show me his infinite love, mercy, and grace. Life was about to get good; really good.

Part 2

From Beer to Bibles

"Make no mistake. **Ron Meyers** is still a promoter. That's what he does best. But on Oct. 25, 1998, he began to change his product from bikini contests and alcohol to the Bible and spiritual salvation.

To Coast residents, a Ron Meyers Production means a weekend of carnival rides, crafts, live music, beer, and seafood but no more. Meyers, once the Coast's highest-profile entrepreneur, is now an evangelist." (Sun Herald, 2002)

Chapter 26

The Birth of Cross 2 Success & My Son

"Before I formed you in the womb I knew you, and before you were born I consecrated you; I appointed you a prophet to the nations."
—Jeremiah 1:5 (ESV)

On the way back from Atlanta, with my mind going a mile a minute, I began to put a plan in motion. With God's help, I was going to form a ministry! Cross 2 Success, a 501c3 corporation, was to be a faith-based success program. From that day forward, things began to get better. They happened quickly both on the inside and the outside of me. My family life was better because the old grumpy, pot-smoking Ron, was gone. We grew closer, my wife and I became active in the Methodist Church, and in January of 1999, we had a visiting preacher in the pulpit from Portland, Oregon. After his sermon, he said he felt led to ask people that needed healing to come to the altar. He would anoint them with oil and pray as the Bible instructs. As I mentioned in an earlier chapter, my precious wife had had a few miscarriages, which was, to say the least, extremely traumatic for an expecting couple. With hope, we both went to the altar. We believed God for another child. A few months later, my wife told me she was pregnant, and this time, I knew without a doubt, everything would be okay. Little did I know just how much my life was about to change once again and that very soon, there would be not one, but two births within a 24-hour space of time.

Cross 2 Success was growing. I had begun holding free meetings every Tuesday night in my offices using the success principles I had already known, but this time—I applied them biblically. I established a phone number which people could call and hear a motivational phone message. It also had an option for leaving prayer requests. This ritual was to go on for several years as every day; I would record a new message and pray for those that had left one. The ministry was beginning to take shape.

One for the first churches to respond was the Assembly of God Church in Kiln, Mississippi. A man by the name of Keith Kaiser called and asked me if I would come to their church the night before our son was to be born and present the Cross 2 Success program. There would be many who would play their part in helping to bring about the success of Cross 2 Success. However, that night, including Keith Kaiser, God introduced me to two more people who would play critical roles in bringing so much to the success of the ministry, Wanda and Emmitt Pillault. That night was truly incredible!

Keith Kaiser, who had initially called and invited me, was to become a close friend and mentor. Keith was a real fireball! He knew the Bible inside and out and would soon begin teaching me everything he knew daily, whether in person or on the phone. I found myself to be like a starving man hungry for every morsel, a sponge eagerly absorbing every nugget of wisdom and truth.

After the program, I met the other two I mentioned earlier who would grow very dear to me and later become my Love Mission Team, Wanda, and Emmitt Pillault. Emmitt Pillault had come up to me and told me that God told him to write me a song called "Cross 2 Success." Surprised, I replied, "That's awesome! Keep me posted!"

The next day, my wife went into labor, and we went to the hospital. They wheeled my wife away, and I was left in the waiting room until called into Labor & Delivery, where I would welcome my third son into the world. To say the least, I was quite excited! While I was waiting on my wife to deliver, who should call but Emmitt to tell me that he had finished writing the song and wanted to sing it to me over the phone! As I listened to the words, I was deeply moved. It was incredible! Below are the lyrics to the song he'd written:

Cross 2 Success

By Emmitt James Pillault

Cross 2 success,
God's plan is best.
Give Him your life today,
He'll do the rest.

God is calling all people across the world
to be what He created them to be.
Come discover God's plan for your life in this life
and you'll get life abundantly.

Cross 2 success,
God's plan is best.
Give Him your life today,
He'll do the rest.

Holy Spirit that raised our Christ from the dead,
guide and inspire me
in discovering all the opportunities
that God has waiting for me.

Cross 2 success,
God's plan is best.
Give him your life today,
He'll do the rest.

I am crossing from my land to the promised land,
The land where God wants you and me to be.
With Christ and me in partnership,
I can fulfill my destiny.

Cross 2 success,
God's plan is best.

Give him your life today,
He'll do the rest.

Cross 2 success.

After I hung up, they came out to tell me that my son was born. Then I heard The Voice say, "Ron, this birth is a symbol of a new life for you."

I responded happily, "Amen!"

Our son, Jacob Christian Meyers, was born on September 9, 1999 (9/9/99). We chose his name so that he would have the initials J.C. as a nod and thank you to Jesus Christ for bringing him into the world safe and healthy. Cross 2 success had also given birth to a new chapter in its growth, which I would never have dreamed.

God's supernatural power ushered in a vibrant, youthful attitude in me. I felt like I was sixteen again! It was as if the heavens opened, and everything was going His way, which was the same way I wanted to be going. There are no words to describe what was happening to me. I had a sincere desire to trust and obey the voice of God and to follow Him on the path to my divine destiny. I have genuinely come to believe that an intimate and conversational relationship with Jesus is the much sought-after fountain of youth. Beyond any shadow of a doubt, I was repaired, restored, and renewed!

Emmitt & Wanda Pillault

This part of the story was based on what was relayed by Wanda Pillault, which gives a little background on the praise and worship leaders who were such an integral part of both Cross 2 Success Ministry and Christmas City USA. Their family has continued to be a part of the success of both Christmas City and Ron Meyers Ministries to this day. Their children and children's children have and still do help with the Christmas City show every year. Their daughter, Maria, who started out helping when she was only a small child by stuffing envelopes, is now the Secretary and Social Media Director for Ron Meyers Productions, and Ron Meyers Ministries.

THE PROMOTER

Emmitt Pillault was an extraordinarily gifted and talented musician and singer who could play just about anything he picked up. He was only 11 years old in the 1970s when he started making recordings in the French Quarter at a studio, then known as Cosmos Studio. A kind gentleman, he was one of those people who loved everyone and made his living playing in piano bars in Louisiana and along the Mississippi Gulf Coast. It was there that he met Wanda, a lovely, tiny blue-eyed blonde from Bay St. Louis with a voice similar to that of Patsy Cline. They sang together one night while he was playing in one of the hotel bars, and after making beautiful music together, they married in 1987. That same year Wanda and her daughter accepted Christ after they attended a John Jacob and the Power Team concert at Victory Assembly Church. Emmitt rededicated his life soon after and gave up piano bars to play instead in Churches.

They joined Cross 2 Success, becoming the Love Mission Team, and would perform in The Warehouse Church and Christmas City, and later would join me at WAOY Christian radio (spoiler alert). Wanda said that people who didn't have anything to do with Christmas City would come from their church service to join in praise and worship and to hear me preach in the early morning before Christmas City would open. A talented Elvis impersonator, Emmitt often used his character to perform in churches, with Wanda by his side. Being also a gifted writer, he changed the words of the classic songs once sung by the original Elvis to magnify Jesus.

In 1992, God told Wanda to tell HR and everyone at her job at Hancock Bank that she was leaving, that God had called her into ministry. She wanted to call her husband, but God made it clear she wasn't to do that. Knowing people would think her crazy, a few people there were particularly religious at the time; still, Wanda obeyed and withdrew all her savings from the bank. She asked God what she was supposed to do with all that money, and He told her to pay off their bills, and that's just what she did. Wanda had always thought she would stay there until retirement and live out her life on the coast as she ever had. She had no idea what she was going to tell her husband when she got home.

When she came home, she found her husband had cooked a beautiful meal and dressed the table complete with candles. Feeling even more apprehensive, she approached her husband.

"Emmitt, I have something I need to tell you..." she began.

"Hi Sweetie—there's something I need to tell you too, but you go first," he countered.

Wanda told him the story of what God had told her to do and how she had quit her job, withdrawn her money, and paid off their bills. Emmitt, very surprised, started laughing!

"Why, Dear! That's what He told me to do as well!" Emmitt blurted, relaying a very similar story. They both had a good laugh and rejoicing; they finished their dinner.

The next day, they set out in their car, not knowing just what they were going to do with no jobs and did as God had told them. City to city, town to town, and from there all over the world, they traveled, preaching the word of God to anyone who would listen. Wanda said that her husband would preach to anyone and anything that would sit still long enough to hear the message. She said she had even heard him once preach to a tree.

"There were times we had no gas," she relayed. "And people would stop us on the street and highway, literally flagging us down to tell us that God had told them to give us money for gas. A few had us follow them to the gas station because they only had credit cards! God always took care of us everywhere we went. When sent to another country, we still had the means to get there, plane fare, food, a place to stay, and home again. We were often mystified as to why we were sent to some of the countries God sent us to, wondering what we would do when we got there not speaking the language, but God always made a way, and we were always well received. We never lacked for anything.

"On one trip through Louisiana, we were stopped by a woman who told us God had told her that we were going to have to stay with her and would be there for several days because a hurricane was coming. We had known nothing about the hurricane. Church members had gone to our home and anointed the entire perimeter of our property, four acres, with olive oil and blessed it, asking for God's protection from His angels from the North, South, East and West. Nowhere that oil touched was a tree harmed, but those in the middle of the property where there was no oil, the trees fell. Our house sustained some damage, but nothing that wasn't repairable, while so many more around us lost everything."

Wanda and Emmitt continued to perform and help with Cross 2 Success and the Christmas show when they were in town, up until Emmitt's death on May 18, 2010.

Chapter 27
Testimony of a Columbine Dad

> I can do all things through Christ who strengthens me.
> —Philippians 4:13 (NKJV)

Mississippi Coast Coliseum
November 3, 1999

> "If all you do is look at the Columbine tragedy, you won't see answers, but if you see through it, you will."
> —Darrell Scott, father of slain Columbine student

Bill Coble, the youth minister of Trinity United Methodist Church in Gulfport, spearheaded bringing Darrell Scott, father of Rachel Scott, in coming to the Mississippi Gulf Coast. Darrell was on a nationwide mission to make sure the meaning behind Rachel's death wasn't lost. On April 20, 1999, Rachel Scott, who was herself a Christian, paid the ultimate price for her faith being the first student to be gunned down that day because she had refused to renounce her faith in Jesus Christ.

I was also a member of Trinity, and Bill asked me if I would do an altar call at this event. "Of course!" I responded enthusiastically. Realistically, I believed I should never have been invited to do this being an untrained minister that was a bit "radical." Not having the degree on the wall, I knew I was one of the "not-good-enough-for-prime-time guys." But what I did have, was the favor of God, and God was about to unleash Himself through me.

THE PROMOTER

Darrell shared passages from Rachel's writings, which were shared up on the giant screen along with several pictures she had drawn that family members say had symbolized what happened at Columbine even before it had happened. The most incredible part of his story was that Rachel had spoken about the end of her life a year before Columbine. She had written in her diary that she was going to die, writing: "This will be my last year, Lord, I have gotten what I can, thank you." According to him, she had written the words, "I'm dying. Slowly my soul leaves. My body withers. It isn't suicide. It is homicide. The world you have created has led to my death." In his presentation, he shared the words she had written when she was 13 years old in a handprint on the back of her bedroom dresser, "These hands belong to Rachel Joy Scott and will someday touch millions of people's hearts." Prophetic words that very much came true.

Further, in the presentation, Rachel's father relayed the story of a man who had called him and told him he had a recurring dream in which he saw tears falling from Rachel's eyes and watering something coming up out of the ground. He had told the man that the dream didn't mean anything to him but agreed to keep his number should anything ever come of it. After the Columbine shootings, he had read the last entry of Rachel's diary on the page on which were 13 clear tears, which had turned to dark drops. He said it had dawned on him that there had been 13 who had lost their lives that day.

He later shared what Rachel had drawn a picture of that morning while sitting in class, which had reflected this same page in her diary, and questioned the teacher about it; but the teacher, Mrs. Caruthers, hadn't answered. At one point, the thirteen crosses, erected in memory of the shooting victims, were brought on stage. The crosses bore pictures of the students and handwritten messages from friends. Some in the audience began to weep.

"If all you do is look at the Columbine tragedy, you won't see answers. But if you see through it—you will," Darrell Scott had said. "Seeing through tragedy requires an ability to look beyond those things that can be physically perceived and to understand that God has a master plan, even during pain and heartache. Rachel's part in that plan was to touch outcasts and those in need with acts of kindness and to reach others for Jesus Christ through martyrdom. She believed if you want to make a difference, try kindness. Rachel wrote in her diary, 'I have this theory that if one person can go out of their way to show compassion, then it will start a chain reaction of the same. People will never know how far a little kindness will go.'" He stopped and looked down a moment, then back out at the crowd, "Rachel started such a chain reaction."

As I was listening to Darrell, though I was captivated by the story of Rachel, I was also incredibly nervous and praying feverishly for the right words to say for the alter call. I had no idea what I was going to say. So, when they gave me the cue to go on stage, I simply said, "Speak through me, Jesus!"

I walked onto the stage, stepping in front of the 13 crosses to see one half of the coliseum packed to the rafters. To this day, I have no idea what I said, but when I gave the invitation to come down to the front of the stage for prayer and salvation, the young and old came, and came, and came. It was thousands. Over half the occupied seats in the coliseum were empty because they had left them to come down to the stage. I don't know if the crowd was reacting to Rachel's story, to something I had said, a combination of both, or perhaps, something else altogether. All I do know is that this time, it had absolutely nothing to do with me. There was little doubt that this was 100 percent, God. I lead them all in a prayer of salvation and renewal, and that night, I literally couldn't sleep for a few days. I was on top of the world honored that God had used me like that!

That evening was the most fantastic evening of my life. I received numerous calls the next day from friends who attended who had told me that night I was glowing and that they had witnessed the beginning of a ministry in which God would use me in a mighty way.

God said, "I will confound the wise with the foolish things of the world." Remember how I had people come against me when I was in the worldly part of my life? Well, soon, much of the church would start coming against me because I was a rebel in their eyes. I'm sure they were thinking, "How could God use a man like Ron Meyers? I am more qualified than Ron Meyers. He doesn't deserve it." You might think I am exaggerating, but I am not.

Chapter 28

The Warehouse Church

> But Jesus looked at them and said, "With men *it is* impossible, but not with God; for with God, all things are possible."
> —Mark 10:27 (NKJV)

In 2000, I closed my offices, which had everyone who knew me calling me a nut. The only event I had left was Christmas City. I was free, happy, and on fire for Jesus. The god of greed that had corrupted my destiny was replaced with Jesus. The Voice that had saved my life on numerous occasions had ignited my divine providence. I was often asked, "How do you know it's God?" My response was, "The first half of my life it was all about me, the rest of my life is all about becoming the person God created me to become. I was blind, but now I see." They were intrigued because they saw a new me, and frankly, I wondered if they were afraid of me. I don't believe they were ready for such a conversion in their life.

I was cutting expenses, so once more, I converted my extra bedroom into an office, and I had to close the warehouse I had been renting. It was still full of the beer booths and Christmas City props; over fifty 4x8 sheets of plywood and one hundred two by fours. I called everyone I knew about taking them free, but no one wanted them. It was disappointing because I didn't know what to do with them. So, I was standing in the warehouse, trying to figure out what to do, and I heard it again; The Voice. That still, small voice inside was saying, "Build a church here. Take the materials and build a church."

I thought to myself, *I've never built anything like that before in my life! How? I don't know anything about construction!* Then I saw in my mind the vision in full living color how it was to look, including the size and even the color of the paint. I said, "Lord, I will, but I want to be involved in a big movement for you."

"You will," said The Voice.

So, for seven days, all by myself, I unscrewed all the wood and began assembling my vision. I built a stage with an altar and had enough material left to contruct myself a little office. I painted it on the seventh day, looked it over, and said to myself, "For someone who knows nothing about construction, this is pretty good!" I couldn't believe my eyes that I'd built this! Now what?

The Least of Them

> And the King will answer them, "Truly, I say to you, as you did it to one of the least of these my brothers, you did it to me."
> —Matthew 25:40 (ESV)

So, there I was, with a warehouse church in a financially devastating part of town. I felt The Voice was telling me to go to the people in the streets, the folks that many of the churches don't want, and let them know that Jesus loves them. Now they would have a place to go on Tuesday evenings and hear about Jesus. Having learned from my early days with the crawfish festivals, I had no desire to cause any conflicts. So, I chose Tuesdays because rumors were circulating that I was trying to lure people from other churches to start my church. Thus, I picked a night when churches were empty.

God was building a community of people who wanted to be loved unconditionally. I went to the soup kitchens, the Salvation Army, and the street people, and invited them on Tuesday nights to come to hear a message of hope, destiny, and purpose. The Voice also told me not to go to the newspaper or television. There was no promotion whatsoever. Invite people personally, period!

During this process, the most amazing opportunities for the production company came my way. Some involved a substantial

THE PROMOTER

amount of money. It was tempting, considering I had just begun my ministry, and funds were virtually non-existent. However, it only took me a few seconds before I turned them down flat, leaving some of them stunned.

"I appreciate the opportunity," I thanked them. "However, I know that God has called me to take my talents, skills, and abilities to advance His kingdom. I must focus on the task at hand, and I can't let money affect my decisions anymore."

To my surprise, they all understood and didn't even try to change my no to a yes. Looking back, I believe those people could feel my passion and vision. I knew my destiny, and I was pursuing it with all my heart. I also thought that Satan was using what had always in the past been my Achilles Heel—money—to deter me from ministry. It took only a few months, and the warehouse church exploded with folks. Preaching in the warehouse was so awesome! It was just an open space, and occasionally, you would see a rat run along the steel beams. When people used the restroom, you could hear them. In the summer, the church was drenched with sweat, and in the winter, bundled up with sweatshirts. But, no one cared. They loved it, and no one complained or said anything about moving.

People often asked, "Why do you think people came?"

I would always reply, "That's easy. It was because we were a bunch of hungry people coming to meet Jesus." I believed Jesus would show up in a big way, and He did!

Every Tuesday, I got there early and prayed. I would have an idea of what I was going to share but was mostly dependent on the Holy Spirit to speak through me. If I was called into preaching, then this meant I was going to put myself in His hands, and He was going to have to show up and work through me, as I knew about as much about preaching as I did about carpentry. I needed Him period. When I listened to those recordings, it was as if I was hearing for the first time. I didn't remember saying most of what I heard. I began recording those messages, and Mark, my sound man, edited them. I bought time on a popular urban radio station every Sunday morning for six months. God was using this wild promoter turned preacher to touch lives radically.

Here is something I feel is so crucial for the church to hear. People are so hungry for what Jesus can do for each of us. Sometimes, the church becomes so polished with sermons or messages that they can miss feeding their starving congregation the bread of life. I may not be the brightest Bible scholar, but I can sure tell you what Jesus did for me and what He will do for you. I have reached so many people with just the words of Jesus. I carry a rock around in my pocket and pull it out to tell people, by myself, I am as dumb as this rock, but with Christ, it is incredible what I can do. I can preach a message with five-second notice. One preacher told me he worked on his sermon for a week. I asked him what if God told you on Sunday morning to preach on something else. His response was stunning, "Oh, that wouldn't happen." I wanted to start preaching to him on the spot about my next message, taking God out of the box, but I was quiet.

I was preaching one evening and made the statement that I don't know why it took me forty years to see the light, but better late than never. After the service, a gentleman came up to me and said, "Mr. Ron, I heard what you said, and you must remember that God trained Moses in the palaces of Pharaoh before He called him out. Mr. Ron, God has allowed you to develop your business skills in the world, and now He has called you to promote him." Wow! That was all I could say besides thank you for the awesome word.

My Favorite Night

My dad was down here for his usual springtime visit. He came to my church service that evening, stood up, and told everyone in there about how I came to visit him in the hospital after he had a carotid artery cleaning, and they could not wake him from anesthesia. While the doctors were on the phone, I strolled into his room. The minute I touched him, he woke up and said, "Hey, kid." The doctors came in and asked me what I did. I said, "I just touched him." They said, "You just saved him from emergency surgery." My dad stood up and said some nice things about me, and we all had tears. Least it appear to you that I am attempting to take credit for this healing, I knew it wasn't me who had saved my Dad; it was God through me who had saved him. I was privileged that He had used me as his vessel that day.

My dad was my hero. There is something that still baffles me. After mom died, he came there a lot. With me having his name, he would love to introduce himself. People often asked him, "Are you the Production Ron Meyers?" He was so proud to say, "That's my son." Here is the baffling part. During one visit, he had carotid artery surgery. Another time he was visiting, he had a kidney removed. Another time visiting, he had a quadruple bypass. However, his last visit would be the one that would rock my world upside down. I believe I know why God sent him on that last visit, which I will tell you about a little later in the story. However, it's always been a mystery to me as to why God sent him a thousand miles for medical care.

A Change Is Coming

It wasn't long before Pass Road Baptist of Gulfport, and the pastor and deacons wanted to meet with me. They liked what I was doing at the warehouse and told me that they owned the church across from my warehouse and would like to let me use it—no more sweating or freezing and watching rats or hearing people go to the bathroom. I was quite excited. It had a nursery, kitchen, sound system, and I just thanked God.

Everyone was so happy and excited about moving. We were a family of hungry people looking for a touch from Jesus. What I didn't know is that God was getting ready to teach me a humiliating lesson about listening, and He would change the direction of my ministry.

My journey from beer to Bibles taught me that you could never be too old, too ignorant, too ornery, too broke, too goofy, or too worldly to be used by God. He can transform even the hopeless into a shining beacon of hope! A man places an imaginary timetable that something must happen by a certain age or that you must have specific training. If you are breathing, then God has an assignment for you. Time is nothing to God. He is not bound by it. This question of time can be hard for us to wrap our minds around since we are finite, and He is infinite. The best way I can explain it is that God operates outside of time. He can do in one day what it might take you or me ten years to complete. I finally realized that all God needs from you is for you to be available and ready and willing to change your destiny, and He'll take care of the rest. I had to stop taking the wheel from Him and be prepared to let Him drive. Yes, it may have taken me 40 years to let go, but do you want to know something? God's timing is perfect. He is always right on time.

Chapter 29
The Brownsville Revival

> God's purpose for my life was that I have a
> passion for God's glory and that
> I have a passion for my joy in that glory, and
> that these two are one passion.
> —Jonathan Edwards

In 1999, I heard about the Brownsville Revival in Pensacola, Florida. The *Brownsville Revival* (also known as the *Pensacola Outpouring*) was a widely reported Christian revival within the Pentecostal movement that began on Father's Day, June 18, 1995, at Brownsville Assembly of God in Pensacola, Florida. Characteristics of the Brownsville Revival movement, as with other Christian religious revivals, included acts of repentance by parishioners and a call to holiness, inspired by the manifestation of the Holy Spirit. More than four million people are reported to have attended the revival meetings from its beginnings in 1995 to around 2000. (Wikipedia)

I had to go check it out. I went on a Friday and was told by several people to get there early, or I would not get in. I arrived at about 4:00 p.m., the doors didn't open until 6:00 p.m., and I was shocked at the length of the line to get in. It was over a hundred yards! So, to pass the time while waiting in line, I began a conversation with some of the other people standing near me and found that most had been here before. I felt all the more intrigued that they had told me they were returning for a fresh anointing of Jesus. The stories they told of healings, salvations, and breakthroughs only made me more excited about my first revival. My Christian journey had taken quite a few twists and turns. I had grown up a Catholic, surrendered my life to Christ in a hotel room, and now I was about to experience something else that I still talk about to this day.

When I finally got in, I wanted to be as close as possible, so I went to the front of the church and was fortunate enough to find a great seat. The lead pastor was John Kilpatrick. But, the worship was led by a man by the name of Lindell Cooley, a Christian recording artist and the leader of The Brownsville Revival in Pensacola, Florida. Never in my life had I heard worship like that! The evangelist was a former drug addict now preacher, Steve Hill, who was on sight the day the revival broke out in 1995.

That evening, I experienced church in a way I had never experienced in my life before or since. I don't remember the details as much as the feeling that if you had a heartbeat and could see, you could feel and see the presence of God. The most amazing thing that happened while I was there was that when I looked at my watch, it was almost one o'clock in the morning. I asked the people around me for the time, and they confirmed it. I had arrived at the church at 6:00 p.m.; however, seven hours later, I was still not ready to leave! I was totally unaware of time and never once looked at my watch during the service! For those who know me, this was indeed a miracle in itself as I have a great deal of trouble staying interested in anything long enough to stay still in one place for too long. That is why I know that the Spirit of God filled that room that night. One lost all sense of time and awareness of anything around them except being caught up in the anointing of God.

The Brownsville Revival became my Friday night ritual. I told my wife since they were going so late, I couldn't drive the two hours home so that I would stay overnight. I believe that this revival is what God used to shape my heart for ministry, broken and desperate people pressing in to get a touch of Jesus. They were never disappointed. It wasn't until after a few months of going that I heard that some of the area churches were there telling people this was a hoax, and it was of the devil. I was stunned to hear such things. I heard it with my ears and saw with my own eyes what was taking place, and I can assure you that Jesus did not recruit Satan to evangelize for Him.

My desire before I leave this world is to see this type of revival again. Only people that attended this can understand what I mean. Going back to the day in the warehouse where I had said I wanted to be a part of the next great move of God, The Voice had said, "You will!"

I have no idea what that means, but I believe with all my heart, God is getting ready to step outside the four walls of the church and turn this world upside down for Jesus. My final prayer before I leave this world is to see 1 million people saved. As I read this for the last edit to be published, I heard The Voice tell me, "You might get a million on your own, but with me, you will get 10 million. Dream big, Ron! I am a big God!" He is right. With God, all things are possible.

September 29, 2000

On Friday night, September 29, 2000, I was in attendance at the Brownsville Revival once again, and God was up to something with me. By this time, I had become friends with so many regulars that we had church before church. There was a point in the service that Pastor Kilpatrick took the microphone and asked all the ministers to stand. Hundreds of ministers stood, including me. He picked around nine to come upon the platform, and I was one of them. He came to me and told me to share what God was doing with me in Gulfport. I took the microphone and looked at a filled room plus the cameras that were televised to the overflow room and on satellite television. I shared about my past days of promoting sex, drugs, and beer to what God was doing today, and the audience erupted with applause. Then Pastor Kilpatrick said, "I have a word for you from the Lord. You are a fisher of men, and God is getting ready to give you a new tackle box with brand new lures!"[1]

"Amen. I receive that in the name of Jesus," was all I could say. That evening was a paradigm shift for me. Just when I thought things couldn't get any better, God turbocharged me!

---

[1] If you would like to see that moment on stage, visit www.thepromotor.org. It is located on the home page.

I remembered a quote I heard from a preacher, "The atmosphere of expectancy is the breeding ground for miracles." Then I thought back to those nights as a young boy, crying myself to sleep and praying, "Please, God, let me be somebody that does great things." I didn't know what God was up to, but it would be something big! I am living proof that He will do exceedingly more than you could ever imagine. I had finally learned that you could never truly love God, know God, serve God, or follow God without an intimate conversational relationship with God. His word is love, in it is power, and there you will find healing.

I recalled my upbringing and the trials I'd been through, and this was my revelation: I believe that it's God's voice that is what's lacking in most people's lives. I can tell you from my own experience, that sometimes I would get so caught up in what I was doing, I couldn't hear him; so busy, I wouldn't see when He was trying to get my attention. Growing up, I was taught many rituals and traditions, but it was never fully explained to me how genuinely personal a relationship God wants with me. He's not just some spirit up in the sky somewhere, some meanie up there looking to strike us down and haunt us with every weight of guilt He can throw around our necks! God wants us to recognize what we do wrong so that we will ask forgiveness for it that we may be free from it. He took it on Himself to pay the penalty for what should have been our condemnation—yours and my condemnation; not His. He asks us to follow Him, not out of fear, but out of love! I find that so amazing, that the God of the Universe who made everything, loves me! Even with my faults, flaws, and shortcomings, He patiently chased me 40 years waiting on me to turn and come to Him. That is amazing! If that's not a God of love, then who is?

I recognized that one mistake that a religious leader can make, which can lead his whole congregation astray, is to be so caught up in the doctrinal opinions and ritual traditions so much so that he misses the entire understanding of just who God is. The Bible warns of this in Samuel 2:27-36, Matthew 15:14; 23: 1-7, John 7:48, Acts 20:30, and Galatians 2:11-16. I believe with all my heart that the only way you can get to know Jesus is through a personal relationship with

Him. He left us a love letter, and within that love letter is life. The Bible is a living document that bears testimony to God's character. It teaches us who He is, how to look for Him and to recognize how creation bears witness of His infinite love and wisdom, His great mercy, and His willingness to take time with even the most minute of details.

Did you know that once they thought the atom was the smallest particle, but with the development of even more powerful microscopes, they've found even more detail within this thing that is so tiny that can't yet be seen? I'm not what you would call a particularly learned man, but if you take the time to just look at the complexity of just how God put things together in the everyday things that you can see, it's just mind-blowing! Take something as simple as noticing how things grow on the side of the road, for instance. Trees stop growing pretty much at the same height. A variety of trees, bushes, and other plants grow together in the wild. Yet, they all grow as if someone deliberately planted them as they come there. So much so, that even the weeds seem part of a giant garden. You would think that though the scattering of seeds, there would be complete chaos, somehow, it all weaves together to form such beauty even in its wildness, that it would be hard for anyone to duplicate.

The love letter I spoke of is the Bible. It teaches us how to be still that we may learn to listen for Him, and recognize that still, small voice, His voice. Through His word, you'll be able to see new possibilities and potential where you didn't think there was any because He'll teach you to open your eyes and listen with your heart. By doing so, you will then be able to recognize and realize the full potential of God, in, through, and around you. God is still very much in the miracle business. He hasn't changed. God is ever the same God as He was in the Bible and He will be the same when He returns. He still speaks to people just like us; you and me. Sometimes, He may use distinct and audible words only you may hear as He did in my case, and other times He may be far less obvious. But when you learn to look for Him, listen for His voice, you will know without a shadow of a doubt when He shows up.

Chapter 30

Time to Open the Tackle Box with My Brand-New Lures

> Then He said to them, "Follow Me, and I will make you fishers of men."
> —Matthew 4:19 (NKJV)

I had a message entitled, "get the hell out of your life." Hell meaning guilt, condemnation, sin, and anything else holding you back from becoming closer to God and discovering His real purpose for your life. I put this message on a cassette tape and made over 500 copies. I had a friend make me fifteen countertop displays that held about fifteen tapes with a sign that said FREE. I felt lead to put them in hardware stores and paint stores where the primary audience was men. Most people had heard of me, so the curiosity factor played a big part. Many had wondered what happened to the festivals and where did Ron Meyers go. Now, they got to hear firsthand. One side of the tape was my message, and the other side was contemporary Christian music. They flew off the counters, and I can just imagine how those conversations went!

"Did you hear what happened to Ron Meyers?"

"Why, no! What did you hear?"

"Well, that old sinner done went and found Jesus!"

Eyes bigger than saucers, "Naw!!! You got to be kidding me!"

"Nope, I heard on this tape he made I got at the hardware store that he shut down the Bikini festivals and everything! No more beer, babes, and barbeque this summer! And what's more, now he's decided he's a preacher!"

"Well, I'll be!"

I'm sure that conversation took a lot of colorful turns. I certainly can't say that at the time that tape caused people to contact me or come to my church service. But later in life, I would meet people who told me stories about that tape. Some told me that I had planted a seed in their heart, and in God's timing, it had taken root in their life. God's timing is perfect.

Sometime later, I wrote a forty-two-page book, *Discover Your Destiny*, and printed five thousand copies to be given to people for free offered through my website. The theme of this book was that God had placed a seed of potential in each of us and that only when we allowed Him to nurture it to grow would we flourish. The book further explained that when a person goes in search of their divine destiny, it ignites a passion for pursuing their purpose with amazing results. The book was very popular, and I received calls for more copies to be used in Sunday school class studies. It wasn't long after I was sending these all over the world.

I wasn't a brilliant author, scholar, or even well-educated. I simply jumped on the potter's wheel and allowed Jesus to mold me into a vessel that brought attention to Him, not me. He put all the right people in my path and made everything happen just the way it should. I believe now, one of the biggest reasons it took me forty years to see the light was that in the past, everything was about me getting attention and my name in the headlines. It took God to humble me and change my heart. I never did anything on my own. All the gifts, talents, and skills I have are because of Him either directly or through those He put in my path all along the way. No man is an island. I was, am, and never will be anything without Him. So, my ego deflated, I have only a desire to promote my friend, my mentor, my coach, my savior, and my everything, Jesus Christ.

Outreaches and the Angel

> "Do not neglect to show hospitality to strangers, for
> thereby some have entertained angels unawares."
> —Hebrews 13:2 (ESV)

The Ministry team and I began going to parks and vacant lots, putting up a tent and serving love, food, and fellowship. People flocked out for the free hotdogs and hamburgers, and they heard music and a message of unconditional love and destiny. At all our outreaches, we sat with folks, prayed with them, and plugged them into local churches. Even though I had a service every Tuesday at the Warehouse Church, I was not equipped to handle all the needs of those we met. Pass Road Baptist Church in Gulfport graciously took a lot of our new recruits for Jesus.

One Saturday, while we were at Henry Beck Park, a sad, run-down park that needed some love, located in what was primarily a low-income part of Biloxi doing an outreach. I was speaking to a small crowd standing and sitting on the grass about Jesus, and out of the corner of my eye, I saw a little, elderly, black woman coming toward me dressed in white. It was fairly obvious she was homeless. Her clothes looked worn and wrinkled; she looked dirty, her hair unkempt, and she was staggering as if she were drunk. I was beginning to feel uncomfortable, wondering what I should do or say to her as she approached me, and to my further discomfort, she stretched her hand out toward the microphone.

"I want to sing," she said, looking up at me determinedly, frowning slightly. By now, I was sure she was intoxicated. But in those few moments that her old brown eyes held mine, something there beseeched me to give it to her. So, I smiled and told her as I handed her the microphone, "I would love to have you sing."

She took the microphone in her small, frail hand, turned to face the crowd, and started singing "Amazing Grace." Quite suddenly, the park went utterly silent. The children stopped swinging, no one moved, and it seemed as even the birds stopped singing, and not a dog barked as time seemed to stop, and all attention was focused on her. As I listened to the huge, angelic voice coming out of this small, time-worn woman, in her tattered clothing with wild hair, I was absolutely floored! She honest to goodness sounded like Whitney Houston! Her pitch was perfect, every note as clear as crystal!

She went through each verse, everything and everyone in the park still silent in complete and utter awe. When she finished singing, the entire park erupted with enthusiastic clapping and cheers. She turned and looked up at me, smiled sweetly, thanked me, and handed back the microphone without any more fanfare than that.

Stunned, I asked her, "Who are you?"

She smiled once again, this time showing no signs of intoxication, and her eyes sparkled as she answered me, "I'm just a homeless person that loves Jesus."

"Well, that was fantastic! I have never heard anything like that before in my life! Would you like something to eat? I'd love to talk to you some more if you'd stick around," I gushed.

"No, thank you, I'm good," was all she said. And within five minutes, we could not find her though we looked everywhere! If you know much about Henry Beck Park, at that time, it was flat and open. There's nowhere to go and nowhere to hide. We all agreed that God had sent us an angel with a message of grace.

Blood on the Tracks
March 25, 2001

One of the most humbling experiences was attending a service for the victims of train accidents at a crossing in Harrison County. That year, in the early part of 2001, eight people were killed in Harrison County train accidents. After reading a newspaper article about a Biloxi animal control officer killed by a train, I felt moved to bring people together in unity to pray for safety and healing. The team got together that Saturday morning behind the Edgewater Mall in Biloxi, and with anointing oil in hand, we anointed the tracks and prayed for the protection of all those who would travel over them from that day forward. Emmitt made eight crosses and brought them to place by the tracks to represent the eight lives lost.

It doesn't matter if ten people or 100 people show up today,' said the Rev. Ron Meyers, 'What matters is that we come together and ask the Lord for protection for people traveling over the railroad tracks. (Sun Herald)

Joycelyn Romero, who lost her son, Emile Desporte, in a car-train accident on August 10, was one of forty people who attended the service by the railroad tracks to pray for the families of eight people killed this year in Harrison County train accidents.

Spirit Fest
April 1, 2001–2004

At the beginning of 2001, it was time to reintroduce my festivals. My newest production would be Spirit Fest, but before I reopened the gates on the old grounds of my heathen days, I felt The Voice tell me to pray over them and redeem the land. I contacted a group of ladies with the local chapter of AGLOW, formerly known as Women's Aglow Fellowship, which is an interdenominational organization of Christian women and men. I asked if they would come and pray over the grounds with me. They came in full force along with their shofar, and we walked the entire perimeter of the grounds that I once promoted Bikini Babes and beer on. For those of you who may not know what a 'shofar' is, it is a ram's horn trumpet used in religious ceremonies by the ancient Jews as a battle trumpet. It is still blown in the Jewish rituals of Rosh Hashanah and Yom Kippur. As all Christianity originates from the Bible, which is a Jewish book written by Jewish people, such customs and traditions often bleed into Christianity, such as the use of the shofar; thus, it fitted that AGLOW included it that day.

Spirit Fest became an annual event each spring, the same timeframe as my once infamous crawfish festival, and ran until 2004. Hurricane Katrina stopped Spirit Fest after that.

To Coast residents, a Ron Meyers Production means a weekend of carnival rides, crafts, live music, beer, and seafood, but Spirit Fest, featured much of the same, yet something was much different…no alcohol. Meyers, once the Coast's highest-profile entrepreneur, now an evangelist, presents Spirit Fest. (Sun Herald)

When I read "evangelist," I had to do a double-take. *How could a number 1 sinner do such awesome things for God?* I wondered. Of course, I knew the answer—by God's love, mercy, and grace. Spirit Fest was a mirror image of the crawfish festival but without the beer and bikinis. I wanted to produce an event that looked like the annual event, but it was filled with Christian music, good clean fun, and lots of love. God saw the need for a family event with no alcohol and used me to produce it. A lot of people said it wouldn't work. Boy, how many times had I heard that? It worked wonderfully!

Live entertainment, face painting, arts and crafts, clowns, and carnival-type delicacies such as chicken-on-a-stick, funnel cakes, hot dogs, lemonade, popcorn, soft drinks, and of course, crawfish. Not a beer in sight!

It was so funny to have people ask, "Where is the beer?"

When we told them, "We did not sell beer," they were shocked!

They never heard such a thing, and asked, "Why would people come to an event with no beer?"

"Sir, the only spirit we want to serve up here is Jesus!"

Many walked away, mumbling, "Stupid Christians, think they know everything. I am not coming back to this. How do you eat crawfish without a cup of beer?"

I just chuckled under my breath.

One attendee said to a reporter, "Take out alcohol and everything not godly, and all you have left is a good thing. People just don't realize you can have fun without drinking. It's nice to spend a day having fun and still remember it the next day!"

I couldn't have agreed more.

Among others, Torrance Small from the New Orleans Saints had come to share his story from the stage, and that evening, I shared my testimony as well. Over thirty people gave their lives to Christ.

God and Country
July 4, 2001

One of the largest Fourth of July celebrations for Christians on the Gulf Coast was The Rick Peden Memorial God & Country Celebration, which had been held on 550 acres, 250 of which were mowed like a well-manicured lawn. Presented were more than a half-dozen Christian artists, many of them local, performing more than six and a half hours. I was invited to come and share my story. On the way to the event, however, I received a phone call from a young man whom I had bought a bus ticket for once so he could go home. He had attended my Tuesday night services in the Warehouse Church, and we had gotten to know one another. He had told me about his situation in which he'd left his wife and come to the coast. After counseling with him, I told him he needed to go back home. He didn't have the money, so I bought him a ticket and put him on a bus back to somewhere in Tennessee. He said he was just calling to tell me to thank you and that he and his wife had visited with their pastor and were now attending church. The rewarding feeling I had received from that phone call put me in the perfect frame of mind to speak that evening.

After I finished speaking, I had an auxiliary sheriff deputy come up behind me. He tapped me on the shoulder, and when I turned around, it was Jerry, who happened to be Jewish; and, by the way, the owner of the Health Club I used to manage. He said that he had no idea I had changed the way I had, and said, "You had those people in the palm of your hand. They were so intrigued by your story. You did a good job, and I'm so proud of you."

Here was the man that had given me my start after the Air Force and allowed me to produce the bodybuilding event as an employee. That entirely made my night—another connect-the-dots moment.

Fire Jam—A Teen Friendly Event
September 2001–2004

Evangelist Ron Meyers of Cross 2 Success Ministries doesn't want his Fire Jam production to be known as just another Christian event that has no relevance to young people. Make no mistake. His message is clearly Christian. But his approach, his message, is about real issues and real situations such as peer pressure, drugs, sex, teen suicide, and violence. "This generation wants someone to talk to their hurts, needs, and desires," Meyers said. "That is what Fire Jam is all about." (Sun Herald)

Fire Jam featured hip-hop, top-selling Christian artists, and then I delivered the message after the music. I felt such a burden to talk to young people about the issues that are leading many of them to drug use, suicide, and running away from home. After all, I had contemplated suicide at age eleven and eventually left home at sixteen. I felt that I could connect with them. So many people and even the church don't know what our young people are dealing with today. It's a tough time to be a teenager. My team was on hand to put them in touch with a nearby church, but the most important thing was to comfort and love them.

I'd like to share with you a sweet message we received after the event from one of the people who attended:

> Thank you, Ron Meyers and Cross 2 Success, for a great Show this past Saturday. Fire Jam 2001 was totally inspiring, as hundreds of teenagers and young adults prayed for our nation, danced with joy and excitement about our future, and encouraged each other with inspirational words of hope and destiny!

There Were Skeptics!

Since I was well known on the coast as the bikini and beer man, a lot of people had questions. "Is Ron Meyers 'real' or is just another invisible con job?" They had seen so many televangelists con people out of money; now they were wondering about me. Even some in my own family, including my brothers, didn't believe I had changed, thinking this was just another con. My wife defended me, but they just didn't know it was possible that I could turn my life around that much. They thought I was too far gone, though they professed to be Christians themselves.

It's incredible when people change their life to something positive about how it is often the very people who are closest to you can be the most skeptical and non-supporting. After a time, I moved on and let my actions speak for me. Perhaps, one day, they will believe that God can transform a person from the inside to become a vessel that brings honor to him. But first, they need to have an encounter with Jesus like I did that will get the 'hell' out of their life. It was sad that in my transformation, I found non-Christians to be more accepting than many of the Christians I knew.

I Closed the Church Services

The transition to the church building was exciting, but two essential things were getting ready to take place and would change my divine destiny once again. Our services were excellent, but it seemed like the attendance was slowly withering away. I would keep plugging away, but something wasn't right, and I couldn't put my finger on it. Even in prayer, I couldn't seem to get any direction from God. I was determined I would fix whatever was broken. I just didn't know God was ready to move me and teach me a lesson.

In October of 2001, I closed the doors to my Tuesday night services. The service had dwindled to almost nobody, and my heart was not into it. I had said earlier that it wasn't going well, and I didn't have a clue why. Before closing, I finally got an answer. I heard The Voice say, "I never told you to move into a church building. You were to be different and not look nor act like a traditional church. People loved the freedom in the warehouse, and I am getting ready to move you."

This was powerful because it was true. I thought since we got a beautiful building, it had to have been God. It wasn't, and I never made that mistake again. I thought when He said move me; I was

THE PROMOTER

going to move away from the coast. I was ready to go wherever He needed me. He was getting ready to push me into the biggest platform I would have for almost ten years.

Those initial years of my ministry were beyond words. God used this untrained misfit to promote Jesus and touch thousands of people's lives with His love, mercy, and grace. The heartbreak to me was that some of the local churches weren't very supportive of what they looked at as my 'Jesus Freak' nature. I just wanted to work with them. I never looked at the ministry as a competition and was hurt by their mistrust. In their defense, I probably would have been a little skeptical of a former promoter that had done anything to make a buck too. However, I knew I should put my focus on Jesus and that my actions would speak louder than words. The Voice said, "Don't let it bother you, Ron. They would like to have what you have: a zeal, a passion, and freedom to do whatever you want within me. Focus on your destiny, not theirs."

Chapter 31

The Announcement that Shocked the Coast

"Therefore, if anyone is in Christ, he is a new creation; old things have passed away; behold, all things have become new."
—2 Corinthians 5:17 (NKJV)

In November of 2001, Roy Wikoff, the station manager at the local Radio Christian radio station, WAOY-FM 91.7, was given additional duties at their parent companies in Tupelo, American Family Association and American Family Radio. For the last four years, he had been the afternoon co-host at WAOY of the afternoon program, "At Your Service," with online personality, Kandi Anderson. This left an opening for a cohost and guess who got the job to fill it? That's right! It came out in the Sun Herald that '...promoter/evangelist, Ron Meyers will host the 4 p.m. slot, scheduled to be expanded to two hours in late January.' If that didn't create a firestorm, nothing would! By opening this opportunity for me, here was proof of just how much God could change a life! I went from cons to Christ in a big, big way.

Below is an email I received written by Roy Wikoff which shows just how much God can intervene:

> "As we go through life, we sometimes have the privilege of meeting very special people. When you do, you just know God is at work. I had

the chance to meet Ron Meyers back in 1994 when I had just taken over as general manager for Gulf Coast Radio. He came in one day and was introduced to me by Katy Taylor, one of our sales reps. Ron was promoting his highly successful Christmas City Show and was placing ads on the radio to promote it. It was also brought to my attention that Ron was the promoter of bikinis, wet T-shirt contests, and sold a lot of beer at his festivals. Later that week, another friend (Bill Sanford) recommended I get to know Ron, and as time progressed, I found myself nearby his office while my daughter was getting dental work done.

Each week or so, I visited Ron in his office, and we talked. I knew there was something special that God was doing and going to do in his life, and I shared that with him on more than one occasion. As time progressed and God started tugging away at his heart, we somehow became pretty good friends. When he started to work more and more toward godly endeavors, I knew he was where God wanted him, even if he did not know at the time.

Fast forward to a time when I found myself needing a partner on the radio show that I was doing on WAOY, and I approached Ron about helping me ask another broadcaster in Gulfport that he knew better than me, and out of the blue at lunch at Chili's, Ron suggested himself as the one. Shocked, of course, I said, "You, you have never done radio." But I knew down deep that it just might be a good idea. He suggested I give him a week or so to prove himself, and if it didn't work out, I could just move on to the other fellow.

"Wow, I did not expect the comments I received from the church community. Ron Meyers? Do you know what he does? Are you sure this is a good idea? But down deep, I knew, and now I know that was the Holy Spirit giving me calm about it. So as time goes by, our friendship grows, and so does Ron's faith and work in ministry. Ultimately, I suggested and made Ron the general manager of WAOY, and the rest is history. I have watched this man grow in faith and work in the Lord, and it is amazing how God is using him even today. So, as I go through life, I count it a privilege to know him and call him my friend."

As Roy said, I had no experience; but, when God calls us, He will equip us and make things happen. Being on the radio was the greatest experience of my life. It gave me the opportunity to reach thousands of people with a message of hope. One of my favorite segments was presented every Friday; it was TGIFFF (Thank God I am Free and Forgiven Friday). I remember the day I came to Christ. It was the most liberating day of my life. The guilt was gone, so was the anger, the bitterness, and the un-forgiveness. I walked out of the prison of self-condemnation into a new and fresh life that now had a purpose and a destiny. I love to remind myself when guilt or condemnation enters my thoughts, *I am free and forgiven!* Removing guilt ushers in fresh ideas and reinforces the unconditional love of Christ. I was getting closer to Him each day because guilt was no longer defeating me in spirit and effecting my thought life.

As you are reading this book, I want to take just a second to share this truth with you as it was taught to me. I believe that too often, we let the devil, or the scars of life, remind us of who we were before Christ. However, what that old devil *doesn't* tell us of is that we are no longer that person! We are no longer bound by those sins, those decisions, those scars. We are made *new*! Hold onto that! When memories arise out of the depths, use that as a calling to

THE PROMOTER

prayer. Thank God that you are no longer that person! Thank Him for His forgiveness! Thank Him for the freedom you now have in Him! What the devil wants to use to harm you, *you* have the power to turn it into praise for The Holy One!

Now, back to the story:

It was important for me to share my freedom as well as open the phone lines, and every Friday, people shared their stories. The overwhelming conversations were that guilt and shame were erased because of faith in Jesus Christ. The stories were amazing, and the faith shared over the radio helped so many struggling. Sometimes, some people were so moved to share their stories; they stopped by the station and shared in person over the air.

I had an open-door policy with the radio station. If you were hurting or needed prayer, stop by. I always had coffee on, and what was the most surprising over the ten years in radio, every so often a person from the past festival days stopped in and said, "Ron, I just about drove in the ditch when I heard you on Christian radio!" Many told me they listened for months, and finally, God moved them to see me. We shared, laughed, and always agreed that we were so young and foolish, but at the same time, God was with us, moving us into our true and divine destiny. Even as I write this book, I find it difficult; because, as you will soon read, one day, my stint at WAOY radio would end abruptly. The WAOY radio community was my family, and we all loved each other. We were a blessing not only to our community but to each other.

God fulfilled a promise. I was rescued as a child, and now His goodness put me in a position of influence and as a light on the coast for healing. Each day, God was using me to send out messages to those who felt rejected, abandoned, persecuted, or lost all hope. I would always pray before I went on air, "Lord, who will we speak to today? Who will be rescued from thoughts of suicide or feel your unconditional love? Use me as your voice. I am nothing without you." There were days when I went off the air after my shift was over after the staff had left, that I would just sit there and reflect the day and my life in general. "Why was I even born?" was my favorite question as a teenager. This question seemed always to dominate my mind, and the Lord would remind me of all He and I had gone through to get where we had arrived. Just as God told me, you too are His beloved child, with a plan. Never forget that.

Chapter 32

Some of My Favorite Stories from the Radio Days

A Psalm of David. "The LORD is my shepherd; I shall not want."
—Psalm 23:1 (NKJV)

Over ten years, I interviewed well over a thousand authors, speakers, evangelists, preachers, artists, and frankly anybody I thought would be of interest to my listeners. It shaped my Christian worldview as well as allowed me to learn from some of the wisest people in ministry. I also learned from real stories by ordinary people. I'd like to share a few of my favorite and most memorable stories I was privileged to be a part of with you from interviews I did during my ten years working for WAOY.

Ashley Smith

In March of 2005, I heard about Ashley Smith, the Atlanta-area woman taken hostage by Brian Nichols. He eventually calmed him by reading an excerpt from "The Purpose-Driven Life" and talking with him about God. I just had to interview her.

Brian Nichols was part of the most massive manhunt in Georgia history. He overpowered an Atlanta courthouse deputy while he was being escorted to court for a rape trial on March 11. Brian Nichols then shot and killed the presiding judge and a court reporter before killing another deputy as the murderer left the courthouse. Later, he killed a federal agent as he fled the authorities. The killer held Smith at gunpoint. He tied her up and then began to converse with her. Ashley pleaded with Brian not to kill her because she was supposed to pick up her five-year-old daughter. As time passed, during the early morning hours at the apartment, Nichols and Smith talked about God, and Brian was becoming more comfortable.

"I asked him if I could read," Smith said. "I got a book called 'The Purpose-Driven Life.' I turned it to the chapter that I was on that day. It was chapter 33. On day 33 of the book, author Rick Warren, a Southern Baptist pastor in California, writes, 'We serve God by serving others.' After that we began to talk, he said he thought that I was an angel sent from God and that I was his sister, and he, a vile murderer, was my brother in Christ and that he was lost and God led him right to me to tell him that he had hurt a lot of people."

He let her leave to pick up her daughter, and she called authorities. "I believe God brought him to my door so that he couldn't hurt anyone else," Smith said.

Eutychus—The Band Perry

There was a local Christian band on the Gulf Coast once called Eutychus, who contacted me about promoting them and playing their music on the radio. Made up three siblings, the group was incredibly talented, and the female singer, Kimberly, was phenomenal. I played their music on the radio and contacted our local mall about showcasing them on a Friday night in the mall. The mall management was at first hesitant about a Christian band, but I believe the favor of God intervened. The mall management gave me approval for their first-ever Friday night concert. The mall was flooded with teenagers on Friday, so this was to be more than just a show—it was destined to be an outreach ministry. Of course, I didn't tell that to the mall folks. The response was very well received, and people loved them on the radio. However, though they had the talent, they just didn't seem to get any breaks. I remember sitting in their living room in Mobile, Alabama, and all of us praying for their success.

One day not long after, the father contacted me and said they were packing up and going to Nashville, where they had some opportunities. I wished them luck, and as often happens with time and distance, I lost contact with them. A few years later, they had a hit song on the radio. Not as Eutychus, but as "The Band Perry"—Kimberly and her two brothers, Neil and Reid. Sometimes, the path we go down might not make sense, but God has the master plan. God ended up using Kimberly and her brothers in a powerful way.

Brittany Waddell—Britt Nicole

I produced a few concerts with a contemporary Christian group called 4-Him. It was time for their farewell tour, and I booked them for Michael Memorial Baptist Church in Gulfport. A week before the event, a friend of mine in Nashville called and told me about a new artist, Brittany Waddell, that had great potential. Could she open for 4-Him? No money, she would just sell CDs. She performed and blew the audience away, and that evening sold over a hundred CDs. Today, she is known as Britt Nicole—one of the hottest young contemporary Christian Artists.

Mercy Me

After the song, "I Can Only Imagine," was released, Mercy Me was in town for a concert, and I had the privilege to interview Bart Millard. One of the questions I asked him was, "When you heard 'I Can Only Imagine' played back after you recorded it in the studio, were you giving each other's high fives because you knew it was going to be a hit?"

Surprisingly, Bart had replied, "Actually, no, we didn't like the song and didn't even think it would be on our CD. It ended up on the CD, secular stations picked it up, and it went to the top of the charts. It was all God." He went on to say that he believed God did that simply to prove they couldn't take any of the credit.

Local Artists of the Week

I started a segment every Friday afternoon that invited local artists to submit a song. I'd play it, then interview them. I didn't spend a lot of time critiquing the music before airing it, and I'm sure most stations wouldn't have played some of the songs I received. The point of this segment was to give these folks a chance to be recognized. All of the people I brought in over the years were so dedicated and in love with Jesus, that instead of being egomaniacs, they encouraged others to walk in their gift. I looked at the station as a community, and if I just looked only for perfect singers, the community would have missed knowing these awesome people who were sharing God's love through songs that most of them had written themselves.

The Bible says that man judges by the outside, but God judges the heart. When some of these songs aired, while the vocals may not have been perfect, you could feel their heart. The world has become so obsessed with everything being perfect that today even many churches want worship artists with beautiful vocals center stage. Many of the "average" people who used to be the backbone of the church choir and once would have often shared solos are never heard. They sit back in their seats, knowing they have a song to sing or a story to share, but they can't because they aren't good enough. So, I gave them a platform for three minutes every Friday.

I prayed for the individuals that have been ignored or told to keep quiet to contact me. Even today, when I hire employees for an event, I have been criticized because I don't automatically choose to hire the best and the brightest. I look at their heart and, most of all, their work ethic. Remember back to my festival days; I hired the homeless because everyone deserves a second chance, or with God—unlimited opportunities. After all, I was one of those misfits myself that most would have thrown away like a piece of trash. I sure wasn't the best or the brightest, but I had a passion for learning, and God always placed someone in my path that always gave me a chance.

The Ten-Thousand-Foot Jump

I once let my attention driven personality get the best of me by talking me into doing something a bit crazy that was picked up by the Associated Press. As I wanted some publicity for the Radio Station, I agreed to preside as the minister at a very dear friend's wedding—three miles above the earth in a Casa Twin Turbine! My good friend Barry Jones Jr. and Dawn Cook told friends they were taking the plunge, and by the fall, they meant it! There in the belly of the aircraft, the Long Beach couple said, "I do." After pronouncing them husband and wife and making one last check of our parachutes, we jumped out to meet family and friends waiting for ten thousand feet below! A week after the ceremony, Barry called and asked if I would marry a couple of underwater assuring me he would take care of getting me certified as a diver. However, I told him I had quite enough excitement for a while, and politely declined.

The Calendar Controversy

You will recall that in my days before Jesus, I told you the story about the Swimsuit Calendar and how I exploited the beauty of scantily clad women to make a buck. Well, in November of 2004, I made the news once again about a Calendar. No, not mine this time, but one that the Hancock County Animal Shelter was producing with scantily clad older women. I was the talk of news and editorial opinions for weeks, and boy did I get hammered! It began when I invited the promoter to do a phone interview on my afternoon show. Here is one of the newspaper headlines and my on-air interview.

> **CHRISTIAN RADIO HOST CONDEMNS FUND-RAISER AS EXPLOITATION OF WOMEN**—Christian radio personality **Ron Meyers** says the Friends of the Animal Shelter is exploiting and degrading women. (Sun Herald)

The animal shelter produced a calendar featuring middle-aged local women. I invited the organization's president to talk about it. Boy, did I ignite a firestorm! Things had come full circle when I found myself now standing in the very shoes of those 'pesky Christians' I referred to back in my festival days. I asked the promoter, "Don't you have any fear of God? You could have chosen another way to raise money."

Did the word *'hypocrite'* bang any gongs when you read this? For many, it did! My point was that I understood more than most about this situation because I had done the same thing years before. I explained, "I understand that 'sex sells,' but instead of the calendar, didn't you think of any other fundraising alternatives?" I even offered to get involved in a joint fundraiser if the group were willing to produce a toned-down cookbook or calendar featuring children.

Here are a few comments posted on the internet.

> **JUDGE NOT**…I want to offer my apologies to Mrs. (Carol) Strohmetz for the way Ron Meyers attacked her. All Christians are not nearly as judgmental as he and other conservative radio people can be. I just hope she wasn't too offended, and all my family and friends will now be getting calendars for Christmas.
>
> Ever heard the old saying about much ado about nothing? Ditto for the calendar in Hancock County. What the preachers need to be concerned about is the high drug and crime rate among the youth instead of worrying about middle-aged women and a calendar trying to raise money for a good cause.
>
> **Ron Meyers** got what he was after when he criticized the calendar girls—publicity. The upside is that he may have promoted the sales of the **calendars**, and that's good. Most of those calling in

took **Meyers**'s point of view. Does it occur to you that the only people who listen to him support his point of view on just about everything?

The Animal Shelter made sure that I knew that the day after the radio interview, that a little controversy goes a long way, and the calendars were selling like hotcakes. They stated because of me; the phones were ringing off the hook. They sold calendars as well as memberships. I was a topic of conversation on many morning radio shows and even on television news. All of them pointed to me as a hypocrite. I simply asked, shouldn't a person who had done a calendar to exploit women be the one voice that, better than anyone, would know how it would bring harm without being attacked? All this controversy did bring more listeners to the station. A lot of people wondered what happened to me after I quit doing the festivals. They had never heard of the station I was on, so we both gained an audience. It was reported that the calendar was used on CBS's *60 Minutes*.

Interviewing folks was very interesting for me. Most would send questions or talking points, but most of the time, I went on my own. I wanted to put myself in the place of the listener and ask those questions they were thinking but wouldn't say. Often, my guest would tell me that I asked questions no one asked before, and they enjoyed our interview. I don't know about you, but I am tired of perfectly rehearsed answers, sermons, or messages. Can we sometimes cut the crap, and let's just talk real? My philosophy worked because since I was friends with all the radio folks on the coast, some would share the Arbitron ratings of stations with me. Arbitron ratings told what stations people listened to and how often. Our station did very well. If I had content that engaged the listener, there was a higher chance they would hear the life-changing message of Jesus. I believe people are getting tired of being lectured. They want real stories that share real struggles with actual tangible results.

Chapter 33
I Become General Manager of the Station

Then the LORD answered me and said: "Write the vision And make it plain on tablets, That he may run who reads it."
—Habakkuk 2:2 (NKJV)

April 1, 2004

Ron Meyers on Air at WAOY, American Family Radio

Since the first day, I was on the radio as a volunteer; I had a goal to become the general manager. For three years, I prayed for God to let me become the general manager. I walked the grounds of the station and prayed that this would be my divine destiny.

I will never forget that day, Tuesday, March 23, 2004, as I was leaving our monthly men's prayer breakfast, I got a call from Kandi Anderson, who had become the General manager after Roy Wikoff had been promoted. She said, "Ron, you know how you have prayed to be the GM? Well, get your resume together because I am going to resign tomorrow. You will be a good manager because you have a teachable spirit, never lose that, and you will do fine."

I got my resume together, and a few days later, I drove up to Tupelo to interview with Marvin Sanders and hired. It is an absolute understatement to say how much I loved that job! I had a mission to share the love of Jesus over the radio. Our station covered approximately a seventy-mile radius. That day, I felt this is what all my past was about. I had come from a life of crazy wild partying through a transformation into a man that God would use on Christian radio. I had been on the air as a volunteer for three years, but now I would be there in a paid position. I prayed hard every day for God to use me.

For the next few months, I made my rounds around the community and called my good friend, Mark, about doing a morning show. He came on board, and I started to assemble the best team possible, and I told them our job was to magnify Jesus across our listening area. The underwriting revenue increased, our listeners increased, and our semi-annual share-a-thon, (listeners call in to donate) exceeded all expectations. I was living my motto, "Do what you love and love what you do!" In hindsight, I can see the hand of God put my team and me in training because we were about to get hit with the worst disaster that ever hit the United States, and God's station would play a vital role in recovery efforts.

Chapter 34

A Storm Is Coming
KATRINA!

> You will not be the same after the storms of life;
> You will be stronger, wiser, and more alive than ever before!
> —Bryant McGill

I was only the GM for sixteen months when I would be challenged with my most challenging test yet, personally and professionally, with Hurricane Katrina. On Saturday, August 27, 2005, two days before Hurricane Katrina, I was at a Promise Keepers event in Mobile, Alabama. Promise Keepers is an event geared toward men about living a victorious life in Christ. I was part of the media team, and around 11:00 a.m., they called all the media to a conference room. They had just got updates from the Weather Channel and decided that they were going to suggest that those in attendance from Louisiana and Mississippi leave. The storm was bearing toward the coast. The way they described it put fear in my heart. After the announcement, there was a mass exodus for the exits. I left, and as I was driving home, I called my wife and told her to prepare to take herself, our two children, and pets to Meridian, Mississippi, to stay with her sister. I asked her to call the hotel in Mobile and cancel my room because I was going to stay at the house so I could be on the scene immediately and get the radio station up for important announcements.

THE PROMOTER

I told her I loved her, but the minute she hung up the phone, I heard that quiet voice turn into screaming not to cancel the hotel room in Mobile. Obediently, I called my wife back immediately. She had already had the hotel on the other line. She apologized to the hotel for the confusion, informing them that I would be returning to Mobile, Alabama, after I had gotten my family off safely to her sister's house. Once home, I helped them pack, kissed them all good-bye, and watched them leave before locking the doors and leaving myself to go back to Mobile. I hadn't packed anything else while I was there because I still had enough for a few days.

With my family safe, I settled into my hotel room. Most of the guests gathered in a large meeting room with other guests, and we watched the devastation unfold over the large screen television. What we saw was incomprehensible. A man in Biloxi was on camera and told how he and his family had climbed on their roof to escape the storm waters. He watched his entire family get washed out to sea. He couldn't save them. They were never recovered. The reports were not useful. Our cell phones lost service; there was nothing we could do, but just sit and imagine the worst.

On Wednesday, after the storm, I had to go home to check on my house and the radio station even though it was against the advice of law enforcement. The whole trip back, my mind raced at what I might find when I got there. I had my media credentials, which were the only thing that got me through several roadblocks. My first stop, of course, was my house. Everywhere you looked, trees were snapped in half or lying on the ground, on roofs and in the streets, their roots upended. Where there had days earlier been homes and businesses, in some places, what was left had been moved from their foundations, with many crushed beyond recognition. Of others, there was nothing left but the slab. What could be recognized as cars, boats, even storage trailers were tossed about as if a child had become bored with playing a game with them. There were pieces of what had once been people's lives littered everywhere. Many power poles had been bent or snapped in half, their lines laying draped about and strewn on the ground and in the streets like steel spaghetti.

The streets were so congested with all of this tragedy; I had to park blocks away from my home. I got out of my car to start walking and noticed something white near my foot. I bent down to pick up the small piece of paper and wiped the dirt from it. It was a photograph of a mom with a child smiling at what appeared to be a picnic. I wondered if they had made it. I finished wiping the mud off the edges and set the photograph down on a washing machine that lay on its side near where I'd parked my car and stood there a moment just trying to process everything around me.

When I finally made it to my street, I saw my neighbor, Kenny, outside and as if on automatic piolet, oblivious to our surroundings, I shouted to him as if I'd just arrived home as on any other day, "Hey, Kenny, how are things?"

There was no explanation for any of our reactions as it was apparent, we were both in complete shock. My cheerful greeting hadn't fazed my friend, who shook his head in disbelief for a few moments before finally saying, "Ron, it's terrible."

I tried to smile, then continued over the obstacle course that had once been my yard towards my house. Finally making it to my front door, I put the key in and turned it laughing at myself as if the lock could have kept the hurricane out. I thought of the scene in the movie *Gone With the Wind* as Rhett Butler was helping Scarlet into the wagon, and she had fretted for not locking the door as Atlanta was being burned to the ground. The door wouldn't budge. I ended up kicking it down and could have never prepared myself for what I saw. Mud was everywhere and on everything. Nothing was left untouched. The refrigerator upside down, and the French doors at the back of the house were blown out. I looked at the waterline, and since we had ten-foot ceilings, I guessed the waterline was at the eight-foot mark. I leaned against the muddy door frame where the French doors had been, starred out into an unrecognizable back yard, and just started crying, feeling utterly helpless. I knew I couldn't fix this. I wanted to reach out to my wife to prepare her for what she would find when she came home, but I had no phone service to report the news.

THE PROMOTER

One of the strangest things I noticed was a bowl of Cheerios sitting on the kitchen table that must have been left there by little Jacob. They were just as dry as if they had just been poured from the box. The table must have floated when the water rose, carrying Jacob's bowl of Cheerios with it until the table rested on the floor once again when the waters receded.

Realizing this wasn't helping, I wiped my face and hands with my shirttail and ran my hands through my hair. I had to plan. In my mind, I had to get back to Mobile. I knew I could get phone service there. I also had only a half tank of gas and had to conserve that. I went in our bedroom and realized I lost all my clothes. No shirts, no underwear, no contact lenses, nothing of the essentials were there. I found a clothes basket and started wringing out filthy mud water from some shirts, jeans, and underwear. Shaking the water out of the bottom of the basket, I piled the wet clothes back into it. I figured I would find a laundromat in Mobile. As I was afraid to use any extra gas, I decided I couldn't risk going to the radio station to check the damage.

This whole time, I am praying for help and listening for The Voice. I heard nothing, yet a part of me still felt peace. I had a house devastated, my family over 150 miles away. I could not communicate with anyone, and I had to get the radio station up as soon as possible so I could give reports. Any peace was a miracle. I was grateful for the hour drive to Mobile to get a plan in my head. The first thing I did was pray to find a gas station and found one. It had a long line, but I was grateful. I prayed the whole time, "Please, Lord, don't let them run out of gas before I get there." I filled up and then was told that the only phone service on the coast was through T-Mobile, so I found a store and bought a prepaid phone and a card to add minutes. I called my wife immediately and briefed her. As you might have expected, she was instantly reduced to tears. I did my best to reassure her and told her we would get through this.

The next thing on my list was to find a laundromat, and I found one right across the street from the phone store. I stared at the window of the washing machine. Watching my clothes twisting in the window, I was reminded of the images I'd seen on television of the violence in the wind and water of Hurricane Katrina. I could almost see it in my mind ripping through the houses where I lived, destroying in hours everything I'd known as comfortable and secure. I could not imagine what would have happened if I hadn't listened and had stayed at the house. I pictured myself struggling in the rising waters and thought about all those poor people who had died. I knew beyond a shadow of a doubt; if I had stayed, I would have been among them. I shook my head to free myself from the terrifying images and decided to think about something else.

I needed to stick to my plans. I had decided that once I got fuel and had spoken to my wife, I would go back to the coast and check on the radio station. It was the next thing on the list. After the clothes were done, I folded them and put them in the laundry basket I'd brought from the house and carried them to the car. Putting them in the backseat, I got in and headed back towards the coast. The radio station was up above I-10, so I was hoping it had not sustained the devastation. Everything below I-10 seemed to have taken the hardest hit. Everything below I-10 looked like a war zone, flattened as if a bomb had gone off. When I finally made it to Highway 49 North, I prayed all the way to the station that it would be in one piece. As I'd hoped, though things were bad, they weren't quite as bad as they had been on the other side of I-10. More of the town was still there. When I turned off the highway onto the little circle where the radio station was located, I saw that engineers from Tupelo were already there, getting us up with a generator. I felt a huge wave of relief to see that the old white house with its small front porch was still there. Many of the old homes had been built by shipbuilders and were strong, having made it through Hurricane Camille. Instead of destroying them when the town began to grow, many were converted to businesses like the one in which WAOY had found it's home. Once again, the shipbuilder's handiwork had weathered another of the most massive storms ever to have hit the Gulf Coast. While some nearby buildings were missing roofs and walls, remarkably, the only damage the radio station had suffered was one lost shingle—God's incredible protection of His station. Since the radio station was in a small house, there was a shower, and I can remember my first shower as I hadn't had one since I'd left the hotel convention in Mobile. It felt like a gift from heaven. Over the next few days, the only food available was from the churches cooking. I ate a lot of things that I would probably haven't touched if I hadn't been so hungry. There were no stores or restaurants left intact. I even ate those little Vienna sausages, which I had never been fond of in the first place. To this day, I cannot look at a can of those little rascals because I relive the days after Katrina in my head.

The Equalizer

I will never forget the day I stepped foot into my home church, Trinity United Methodist, in Gulfport for a hot meal after Katrina. In line were bank presidents, lawyers, teachers, construction workers, and a state supreme court judge. We all had the same story. We had the shirts on our backs, and the lucky ones had a few extra. We had no food and no way to communicate on the coast. I remember thinking as I was waiting in the food line; it didn't matter how much money a person had; it could not fix the problems in those days after Katrina. Big or small, rich or poor, we were all helpless but for the grace of God that brought in thousands of relief teams and workers.

Here is something that will make you think if you are a skeptic of God: I eventually would interview many of the relief workers and asked them, "What made you come here to help us?"

They heard "The Voice." They were doing their thing, safe in their worlds, but when they saw the news, they heard loud and clear, "Go help my children." They all said they never even thought twice. To help perfect strangers, they dropped what they were doing, packed up their trucks, their cars, trailers, and campers with tools, food, blankets, everything they had to share, and headed South. And not just a few people, an army of people came, and came, and came! God is so good that He sends people to you when you go through a storm.

Here Come the Campers

Word got out through the national broadcast by many ministers, including myself, as the station manager, about those who lost our homes. Within days, over twenty-two campers came to the coast and were given to preachers. There was a sweet couple from Kentucky who brought my family a camper and set it up in our driveway. They handed me the title and said, "This is yours, and may God bless you and your family as you rebuild." I was astounded! For a few moments, I was so overwhelmed; I couldn't say anything. When I found my voice, I thanked them profusely. Amazing love by God's children!

The next few months were quite astounding. The radio station became a hangout for people coming to the coast to help. They camped out on the floor at night, we made breakfast on a grill in the morning, and we sent teams all over the coast. They went out to meet people who lost everything. The grace people showed through the disaster impacted my life tremendously. Not one person whined or complained. They were grateful to God for sparing their lives and so appreciative of the tents, sleeping bags, or cans of potted meat and bottled water we gave them. When I became the station manager, I developed a theme, "WAOY—The light of the Gulf Coast."

We were the light of the Gulf Coast. Every time we went on air and said what our needs were, they came. I was interviewed daily by the staff at headquarters in Tupelo. Our plight was broadcast to over 175 stations. For weeks upon weeks, people came in to share their stories and God's remarkable provisions. These stories were life to those who did not believe in God. I heard first hand the stories of how many people became Christians through this outpouring of love from other Christians all over the world. One of the most heard stories from relief teams was that they came here to help and serve the community. But by making themselves available and loving and serving others, they were the ones that were blessed. I interviewed many groups that came back every six months as well as countless others that packed up and moved to the Gulf Coast. It is in times of tragedy that God's people come alive with his spirit of love and compassion.

THE PROMOTER

One particular day, a person came to the station and asked to speak with me. I brought him in my office, and he proceeded to tell me that he appreciated all that I was doing to help the community come back. He then said something that reminded me of the story I had been told a few years before in the Warehouse Church about Moses being trained in the palaces of Pharaoh before God called him to do his work. He said, "Ron, do you realize that God had trained you with all your organization and public relations skills for this time in your life? You are leading the Christian community during this time. Your encouragement on the radio is the only thing that is getting some people through the day. I just felt the Lord told me to tell you that because I know you lost your home, and yet you are here every day sharing God's love."

I had tears in my eyes and told him that I was so appreciative of his coming by. I told him what the people don't know is how much I was hurting for the coast. I told him I couldn't even drive on the beach because the memories of so many beautiful places my family experienced were wiped away and would never return. I went on to say that every word I speak on the radio must be a word of hope or encouragement. To be honest, I was talking to myself most days.

I walked him to his car, and as I came back, I had this revelation from God. I was reminded that all the facilities that hosted my events were gone. Now, as general manager of the station, I had an income to support my family; otherwise, I would have had to leave the coast to look for a job. I heard The Voice say, "God knows our past and knows our future. He is always looking out for us."

I must tell of another divine appointment from God. Before Hurricane Katrina, a young lady by the name of Beth Hester was organizing the Christmas City show. After Katrina, the coliseum was under renovation, so no Christmas City for 2005. I hired Beth at the radio station, and she was an absolute angel. She was the hands and feet for many of the relief efforts. She met planes at the airports full of supplies and organized distribution points, contacted churches, and so much more. I called her the angel from God. I got a lot of credit for things, but I was quick to point out that Beth Hester was the behind the scenes person. We had an incredible team.

Dana Wittmann, who was our representative for recruiting underwriters for the station, had a ministry bus that we loaded up daily with water, tents, food, and prayer teams that went from one end of Mississippi to the other, delivering these supplies and praying for people. We seemed to have a constant supply of supplies. I would tell listeners on-air what we needed, and within hours, it was at the radio station.

My Contractor

> "Beware of false prophets, who come to you in sheep's clothing, but inwardly they are ravenous wolves."
> —Matthew 7:15 (NKJV)

During the aftermath of Hurricane Katrina, a contracting company came to the radio station and offered to put blue tarps on people's damaged roof to protect them from the rain at no cost. They sure liked to say Jesus a lot. During our conversation, I ended up hiring them to rebuild the inside of my home. My structure was fine, but everything had to be gutted and put together again. The situation became an ordeal—what was supposed to take four months ended up taking over nine months. After the construction company had finished rebuilding our home, I was looking over my receipts one day and realized they overcharged me around twenty-five thousand dollars. Instead of contacting them, I went straight to my attorney and filed a lawsuit.

They came back with a countersuit claiming I underpaid them twenty-five thousand dollars. As a result, we ended up in court. After days of testimony, the judge ruled in favor of the contractors. I was shocked and furious. I told my attorney I wasn't going to pay. First, I didn't have the money, and second, it was an unjust verdict. For the next four years, I avoided the entire situation and blamed myself for acting too hastily. They had a brilliant lawyer that was way more prepared than my attorney. So, I went out of my way to avoid them. I still remember going into grocery stores and looking down aisles to make sure I never ran into them. It was four years of living in fear.

I felt if I ignored the situation, it would go away. Eventually, the amount of money they stole from my family wasn't worth it. I called my attorney and said, "Pay them. I can't live like this anymore." It ended, finally.

The Rest of the Story

God was teaching me something. A few weeks after I paid them and put it out of my mind, I received an application for a booth in my annual Christmas City gift show. It was the contractor's son. He and his wife wanted a booth. My immediate thoughts were, No, absolutely not!! After a deep breath, I heard The Voice, "What would Jesus do?" If God was testing me, I was going to pass the test with flying colors. I gave them the best booth available, and I was compelled to pray for them. I dreaded seeing them at Christmas City that year, but God was setting me up for a life-changing lesson on forgiveness.

At Christmas City, I avoided them entirely until Sunday morning. I conduct a church service at Christmas City. When I finished the service, I was walking towards the information booth, and I saw them in their booth. I had a choice to walk away from them or pass in front of them. I bet you know what The Voice told me to do; yes, walk in front of them. The minute I got in front of their booth, the contractor's son stopped me and said, "Ron, I want to thank you for letting us in the show, and that was a good message."

I reached over and shook his hand and said, "Thanks for coming, and I am glad to have you. Your wife has beautiful items."

The second I touched his hand, The Voice said, "Father, forgive them for they know not what they do."

Wow! The real 'wow' was that I started feeling sorry for them. That day I experienced the power of forgiveness that changed me forever. I never understood why God allowed them to win, but today I think I know. It was more about me not talking to them before filing a lawsuit. I believe it would have been worked out if I had reached out to them before going to a lawyer. That Sunday, the anger, bitterness, and resentment melted like a sandcastle beneath a cascade of water. I discovered that God needs us to be free so that He can impart more of Him in us.

I strongly encourage you to look over your life and start making a note of those people who you have an issue. Don't allow anger and bitterness to block the wonderful life God has for you. He will deal with people who have come against you. You have so much to offer the world, and Satan would love for you to become stagnate with bitterness. This is your time, and if God healed my hurts, He will most certainly heal yours. One of my favorite prayers is "Lord, search my soul and show me anger, bitterness, or resentment that is stopping me from my divine destiny. Please forgive me as I forgive those who have wronged me. Take any baggage that I am holding onto and burn it, Amen!"

Chapter 35

Terminated!

> "But I am afflicted and in pain; let your
> salvation, O God, set me on high!"
> —Psalm 69:29 (ESV)

It was Tuesday, November 23, 2010, and I was conducting business outside the radio station when I received a call from my office. The office manager asked me if I had been at my home, and I told her no and asked why. She said I should go there, and there would be a FedEx package for me. I rushed home, and sure enough, there was a package lying against my door. I opened it up, and the next few sentences changed my destiny. "Your job is being terminated. The local station is closing."

I thought, *Terminated, isn't that a movie with Arnold Schwarzenegger?* I immediately went back to the station, and all the employees had received the same package. But what I didn't see in the package was a severance package, which was very generous; however, it stated that if we mentioned this on the air or contacted the press, we would lose our severance package. It meant that I would just disappear from radio, and never be able to tell my listeners goodbye. That day, I went through with my regular show, happy and inspiring as usual, but when I turned the microphone off, I knew I would never return even though I had a few weeks remaining. I couldn't do it. I would have been too emotional during my show.

The Loss Was Worse than Death

With death, it's over—period. This loss would linger and will be with me for the rest of my life. It was a loss that has no words to describe. My listeners had become my friends and family. I had an open-door policy, and often people would come by to talk and receive prayer. What was I to do? What was my future? I had walked away from the production company, but I still held onto The Christmas City Gift Show. That could support me until I figured out what to do. We had thirty days to clean out the office, and when the engineers came to tear down the studios, I had to go outside and cry. I was angry at God. I couldn't understand why this was happening. Our station had been in the top three with revenue and listeners, so it wasn't the economics. It was explained to us that corporate was going in a new direction and that a national broadcast would replace the local stations across the country. How could a national radio broadcast help our community? Who would be there to encourage those who were hurting? How would local ministries and churches get information to our community? How could God let this happen?

I know I needed an office for starting all over again, so I reached a lease agreement with Corporate for the little white house that at one time was the radio station. They sold me all the desks, chairs, and equipment for a nominal cost, and I would begin my new career, whatever that was going to be, in the shadows of my favorite part of my life. Do you know that even today, when everyone is gone, I sit in the room that used to be the studio, reliving those interviews? One was when I interviewed Billy Graham's minister, Don Wiltshire. I asked him at one part of the conversation if when he saw Reverend Graham, would he ask him to pray for us. I didn't even complete the sentence when he said, "Ron, Billy has been praying for you and the folks of the Gulf Coast." Wow, I was blown away! I sure hope he was still praying for me.

To those who have been terminated for no fault of their own, let me say, I am so sorry. It is a feeling that I wouldn't wish on anyone. I questioned myself and my talents. I had never been terminated before, and I believed I was going to be involved with radio until the Lord called me home.

THE PROMOTER

In the weeks that followed, I just walked around in a daze. One day, sitting in my office, staring at the walls in a room so quiet, you could hear only the old floorboards creaking and popping, I said out loud, "Why, God? Why would you stop all the work we were doing? What am I going to do?"

The Voice answered crystal clear. "Ron, your title became your identity with that of your occupation. You were a general manager, an on-air personality. You introduced yourself that way at functions and signed your letters that way. You even had a sign on your office desk with your title. You loved your title so much that your title became your identity. You became so obsessed with it that you barely listened to me and only listened to yourself. You even stated that they would have to pry your dead fingers off the microphone. You unknowingly changed your identity from 'child of God with a divine destiny' to 'arrogant manager who knew it all.' When you shed your identity as a child of God following my destiny for you, you closed the door of communication with me. You would tune into your station, but you weren't tuning me in. Let me ask you a question, would you have left on your own? It was time to move you. One door must close before I can open another door."

Boy, did that knock me off my pity pot. I was humbled and felt ashamed. I would have never left on my own, and I did say one time on the air that I loved my job so much, they would have to pry my dead fingers off the microphone. That was an arrogant statement. Now I had to trust God more than at any time in my life. That is much easier said than to be able to do. The words from my early days kept ringing in my ears, "You're worthless. You screw up everything you touch."

Perfect Timing

One day, I went to the gym for some exercise, and I ran into a friend I hadn't seen in a few years, and wouldn't you know, the first thing he asked was, "Ron, why haven't I heard you on the radio lately?"

I was brief as not to violate my severance package. This friend told me that he had something in his gym bag he wanted to give me.

It was a book by Mark Batterson, *In the Pit with a Lion on a Snowy Day*. I opened it up, and the first words I read where "God is in the business of strategically placing us in the right place at the right time even though we may think it is the wrong place and the wrong time." He went on to encourage me with things like, "Ron, I hadn't seen you in years, and today, I run into you with a copy of this book in my gym bag. That is God, Ron. He is moving you into something else."

But I didn't want to be moved into something else. I lost my 401K, my insurance after the severance package ended, and I was not prepared to go back to productions. I thought for the longest time that I would receive a phone call that Corporate made a mistake, and the station was coming back. I never received that call. Now I had to practice the very thing I preached on the radio the past ten years—Let go and let God. I decided I would begin looking for a radio job. I picked the states of Florida or Texas. I was getting excited, but God wasn't going to let me go. He was getting ready to make me take a seat and sit still for almost eight years.

For the next few months, it was so difficult to go places and have people recognize me or my voice. I couldn't talk about it, not because of the severance package. I got emotional because I lost my radio family. I couldn't tell them goodbye, or I love you or until we meet again. My community of people who I loved, and they loved me. Today, I know good things came out of it, but it is the only thing in my life that I truly miss and still hurts. I lost my true love, and it was totally out of my control. It will never go away, and when we lose a job, friend, loved one, or pet, it will hurt forever. Just do what I do, remember the memories, and hold even tighter to the hand of Jesus and pray each day you get stronger.

I will end this chapter with some advice. Always remember what your most important title is, Beloved Child of God with a Divine Destiny. Be prepared for changes. Never get so comfortable in your current title that you close the door of communication with God. It worked out for me. Today, I can see that one year later, the worst day of my life became the best day of my life—even though I miss my radio station days—A LOT!

Chapter 36

God Sent My Dad to Me

> "But if anyone does not provide for his own, and
> especially for those of his household, he has denied
> the faith and is worse than an unbeliever."
> —1 Timothy 5:8 (NKJV)

Each year from January to March, I would bring my father down here to golf and get out of the snow. His official nickname was Snowbird. In 2010, about a month after the radio station closed, Dad called about coming down after Christmas. We decided that he would head South on January 10, 2011. As we were talking, he told me how he slipped on the ice as he was taking the neighbor's trash out. That was Dad, always helping the neighbors. He told me he hit his head, but that he was okay. I told him to go to the hospital and get checked, but he still insisted that he was okay. So, I suggested that he come early for his visit, leave a few days after Christmas, to get out of that crazy weather.

He left the cold, icy Iowa weather on his birthday, December 28th, arriving a few days later in perfect weather. He didn't waste time hitting the golf course, and he appeared to be thoroughly enjoying himself. But on Saturday, January 10, he started saying the silliest things, and I told my wife that something was wrong. I took him to the ER, and the doctor came out and asked me if my dad had fallen recently. I told him the story, and he said, "Your father has a subdural hematoma and has to have emergency surgery."

Wow, another game-changer. The doctor said if I didn't bring him in today, he probably would have never awakened. I had to sign all the consent forms, and when I put in the date, it hit me this would have been the day, January 10, 2011, he would have been on the road driving one-thousand miles—God's favor once again, this time on my wonderful father.

The next four months were traumatic. We didn't know if Dad would make it. He never fully recovered and wasn't going to be able to return to Iowa, where his friends and the rest our family lived. This meant he was going to stay in Mississippi, where he became a resident for Medicaid reasons and where he would remain for the next eight years. I knew I couldn't leave my Daddy, so I shelved any ideas of looking for a job out of state.

He was going to require more care than I could give him, forcing us to find a place where he would get the expertise of care and attention I couldn't offer. When it was time to find a nursing home, there was only one I wanted him to go—Lakeview. I had heard so many good things, and it was within five minutes of my office in Gulfport. The social worker informed me that there were no openings, and he would have to go somewhere else. I told her, "Let's just see what happens today."

My first thought was, *who do I know that could help me?* But I instantly knew I had to go to God. I remember my desperate prayer. "God, I need help, you have to get him in Lakeview. Please, and it needs to be today."

A few hours later, the social worker called and said, "Mr. Meyers, good news, Lakeview just called, and they will be taking your dad."

I had only three words, "Thank you, Jesus."

I had forgotten she was still on the line when I heard her chime in, "I agree!"

Dad was the life of the party. The place was populated mainly by women, and as my Dad was a real charmer, they liked Dad. Of course, he enjoyed their company as well—all of them! At times, my Dad could be a real charmer; but overall, he usually behaved himself. I was up there visiting him all the time.

On one visit, a nurse said, "Your father is very fortunate."

"Why is that?" I asked.

"Because you're here all the time," she looked at me kindly and smiled.

I looked at her, surprised, and replied, "I didn't know there was any other way to be. He is my Father, and I will do whatever I need to do."

She went on to tell me that most of the patients only see their family at Christmas. When she left, I took my dad's hand and said, "I would never do that to you, Pops!"

A few minutes later, while thinking about what the nurse had said, The Voice said, "A person that doesn't respect their earthly father will never respect their Heavenly Father." I thought, so true.

The Power of Love

One day, I was walking down the hallway focused on getting to Dad's room, I hesitated as out of the corner of my eye, I saw a lady sitting in a wheelchair with her head slumped. It was as if a magnet was pulling me to her. I didn't have time for a visit. But I walked up to her, gently touched her shoulder, and said, "Hi."

She perked up with the most beautiful smile and said, "Hi, who are you?"

I felt chill bumps everywhere. I said, "I'm Ron, and Jesus loves you."

A nurse witnessed this and said, "That lady hadn't said a word or smiled as long as I can remember. You have a magic touch."

I visited a few minutes and walked back to Dad's room. I thought what was that all about, and I heard The Voice say, "Love."

It took me a few days to figure that out. As we all are when we allow God to work through us, it dawned on me that I was acting as a conduit of God's love. From that day on, I would intentionally talk to at least one person every time I went to see Dad. I found this incredibly rewarding! Unfortunately, on too many occasions when I missed someone and inquired where they were, I found they had passed. It made me realize that I may have been able to give someone the love and attention even in that short amount of time they may have left, that they may have needed to feel they mattered. The nursing home taught me to appreciate life.

For We Know Not What Day

After seeing my visit with Dad one night, I remember walking down one of the long halls with its rows of many doors. Behind each one lived one or more residents of the nursing home, which at this time of the evening, would be lying in their beds. It was well after supper, somewhere around 9 p.m. or so. I couldn't help but notice the sound of a television playing very loudly coming from one of the rooms. A commercial was blaring through the hallway, "Bring in your cola can for $20 off your ticket price this weekend at Blue Bayou Water Park in New Orleans, Louisiana!" As I drew nearer to the room the noise was coming from, I stopped momentarily in the hallway just out of sight and peered through the doorway to see a thin pair of very frail and very pale looking legs belonging to a man lying on his bed. I wondered if his loud set bothered anyone else on the floor. I had no plans to bother him but continued on my journey to the double doors and, on arriving, pressed the large button on the wall that would signal the nurse to unlock them and let me out. As expected, I promptly heard the loud click as the bolt slid out of the way to release me from the nursing home. But as I raised my hand and placed it on the large, heavy, thick wooden door in front of me to push it open, it suddenly hit me with the force of a locomotive that I had just witnessed.

Most of these people locked behind these doors would never see a water park again, or any other park for that matter. Many would never again hear the laughter of children, smell and taste of cotton candy, or stand on the peers and enjoy the salty spray in an ocean breeze that was only a little way from here. Some would never be able to come out to enjoy the flowers planted in the front of the nursing home, mainly for the benefit of the visitors. They would never hear the song of crickets, the wind in the trees before a storm, or see the stars in the sky again. Many of these people would never again even feel the sun on their face, the arms of a child, nor something as simple as a kiss on their brow by someone who cared about them. How many were rarely ever visited or had just been left there to die, unwanted? It dawned on me as much time as I spent there, that there were far too many that I never remember having seen anyone come to visit them. As I thought about these things, my eyes welled up with tears as I made my way to my car. I got in my car but just sat there for a moment with my hand on the ignition key. I was about to leave from this place, stop where ever I wanted for a meal while they were at the mercy of whatever they were fed. I could stop to see a friend, while they lay trapped in their beds, helpless and alone. All those things we take for granted, they had lost, trapped behind those doors, prisoners that their bodies had forced them to become. As the tears I'd fought spilled down my cheeks, I took my hand off the key, and lay my head across the steering wheel. I knew I would never again take anyone or anything for granted ever again.

Dad's Last Wishes

Saturday night with Dad and Lawrence Welk became a norm. He loved it, and often, he would sing out loud, and I thanked God silently as he sang that I had another day with him. His favorite show was Andy Griffith; he loved Barney Fife. He laughed all the time. He loved it when my wife brought him cookies. He always greeted me with, "Hey, number one son!" But when my wife went up there, you would have thought he had won the lottery. He called her "the best daughter in law ever."

Santa, Ron Meyers Sr. and Ron

Dad always said he wanted two things before he died. One was that he lived to eighty-four, and the other was that the Chicago Cubs win the World Series. I was fortunate to be with him the night the Cubs won, and boy was that a rewarding moment. My Dad got both of his wishes. For the eight years, dad was in the nursing home, he never missed my Christmas Show, and I made sure Santa always paid him a personal visit.

I am so grateful to St. Joseph's Catholic Church for the love they showed Dad. Every Thursday, two ladies from St. Joseph's visited him, gave him communion, and prayed with him. He loved his church.

The Election

One of my last memories with dad was in November 2016; I ran for a state senate seat. Even though dad was a diehard Democrat, and I was running as Republican, he was so proud to wear my sticker, Ron Meyers, for State Senate. My work ethic came from watching my father as I grew up. I remembered those weekends he would take us boys to work with him. I mentioned he did janitorial work, and it was from him we learned to work with excellence. He was a good man, and I am blessed to have his name.

When I ran for the State Senate Seat, I frequently heard, "If it's God's will, you will win" and "Don't run if it isn't God's will." So, I began asking myself, "What is God's will for me? Will Jesus knock on my door and tell me to run? Will He call me on the phone and tell me not to run, or will He just send me an email?" I know that sounds facetious, but I honestly wondered just how would I know?

Here is what I believe God's will is or isn't. God's will isn't necessarily realized through the receipt of awards, jobs, or relationships. Sometimes we pursue those things hoping to receive them. His will is, regardless of what happens, that we keep moving forward, not standing still, becoming complacent, and, most importantly, that we pray for guidance and forward movement. We shouldn't associate God's will necessarily with whether we win or lose, as much as we should with the definition of the path toward our journey. After all, some of the greatest lessons, the greatest blessings come with losing, not winning, or that relationship not working out instead of finding out you've tied yourself to someone that brought you misery. Some of God's greatest gifts indeed are unanswered prayers.

It's been my experience that most people, often "talk big" but do very little. Christians, however, like to use the excuse when we cop-out or quit, "Well, I guess it just wasn't God's will." While in some instances, this may indeed be the case, more often, we are not always willing to put forth enough effort, faith, and courage to pursue the ideas God gives us. After all, if we aren't faithful with the little things God gives us, why would He give us the big things for which we pray? He will not. Why would God give us ideas and ministries and then say, "Oh, never mind, I was just kidding." He wouldn't. Therefore, we must stop blaming our shortcomings on God's will or a lack thereof. Learn from the experience and keep moving forward. As I said, life isn't about winning or losing but getting in the game of life. I did not win the election, but I worked hard to be obedient to what God called me to do, and I loved every minute of the experience, regardless of the outcome. I didn't mind losing as much as I thought I would because this had reminded me that the world needs more Jesus, not more politicians.

I said earlier in the book that I didn't know why God sent Dad here when he needed medical attention, particularly for the last eight years of his life. Perhaps it was to give me what I missed as a child. Except for this time, the roles were reversed. I had the honor and pleasure of taking care of my dad. At times, I had the arduous task of watching Dad suffer and begin to deteriorate right before my eyes. That was very difficult.

The Last Good-bye

On Wednesday, August 15th, the nurses called and said that hospice was taking care of my dad and that it would be just a matter of days. When I arrived at the nursing home, I told Mama Bear, Dad's excellent nurse, that I expect God to bring him home on August 19th. She asked why, and I explained, "Because that is Mom's, his wife's birthday. As predicted, my Dad did pass on my mom's birthday, August 19, 2018, and he was taken home to Iowa to be laid to rest next to Mom. I conducted the service. My message was that Dad never once in eight years complained or said, "Why me?" The nurses and residents loved him, and he was kind to everyone. He preached the greatest sermon each day through his actions: love, respect, kindness, and faith. It didn't matter who they were or where they came from, whether they were white, brown, black, purple with pink polka dots—Dad loved everyone. I told the folks in attendance at the funeral that in a few weeks, you may not think of Dad as often, but if you are kind, loving, and respectful to others, you can still share Dad with others.

For those eight years with Dad, I had put some things on hold and deferred job opportunities in other markets. But I believe God needed to teach me something about relationships before I could finish this book. Caring for parents and children can be challenging, but the ability to see past the challenges and embrace relationships is priceless. Jesus taught us that without regret, we must love, forgive, love, and forgive. If we cannot encourage, empower, or inspire with our words, perhaps we should remain silent. Most of the time, our actions speak louder than words. St. Francis of Assisi said it best, "Preach the gospel everywhere and when necessary, use words."

It has taken some time for me to get used to not going to visit Dad. I can't watch Lawrence Welk yet, but one day I will so I can reminisce about him singing along. Driving back from the funeral, while realizing I have some pretty big shoes to fill. I knew that it was time to finish writing this book.

About the Author

Writer, radio host, and inspirational speaker Ron Meyers is passionate about promoting destiny. He is the author of a children's book, **Little Johnny and The Voice of Truth** *and a self-help book,* **Get the Hell Out of Your Life**. *Ron loves to encourage, empower and inspire individuals to live life out loud!*

CPSIA information can be obtained
at www.ICGtesting.com
Printed in the USA
FSHW011806011020